Cambridge Elements

Elements in New Religious Movements
Series Editor
Rebecca Moore
San Diego State University
Founding Editor
†James R. Lewis
Wuhan University

YOUTH CULTURE AND RELIGION IN TWENTY-FIRST CENTURY JAPAN

From Hyper-Real to 2.5-Dimensional Religion

Satoko Fujiwara
University of Tokyo

Hiroki Miura
University of Tokyo

CAMBRIDGE
UNIVERSITY PRESS

Shaftesbury Road, Cambridge CB2 8EA, United Kingdom

One Liberty Plaza, 20th Floor, New York, NY 10006, USA

477 Williamstown Road, Port Melbourne, VIC 3207, Australia

314–321, 3rd Floor, Plot 3, Splendor Forum, Jasola District Centre, New Delhi – 110025, India

103 Penang Road, #05–06/07, Visioncrest Commercial, Singapore 238467

Cambridge University Press is part of Cambridge University Press & Assessment, a department of the University of Cambridge.

We share the University's mission to contribute to society through the pursuit of education, learning and research at the highest international levels of excellence.

www.cambridge.org
Information on this title: www.cambridge.org/9781009550222

DOI: 10.1017/9781009550239

© Satoko Fujiwara and Hiroki Miura 2025

This publication is in copyright. Subject to statutory exception and to the provisions of relevant collective licensing agreements, no reproduction of any part may take place without the written permission of Cambridge University Press & Assessment.

When citing this work, please include a reference to the DOI 10.1017/9781009550239

First published 2025

A catalogue record for this publication is available from the British Library

A Cataloging-in-Publication data record for this Element is available from the Library of Congress

ISBN 978-1-009-55026-0 Hardback
ISBN 978-1-009-55022-2 Paperback
ISSN 2635-232X (online)
ISSN 2635-2311 (print)

Cambridge University Press & Assessment has no responsibility for the persistence or accuracy of URLs for external or third-party internet websites referred to in this publication and does not guarantee that any content on such websites is, or will remain, accurate or appropriate.

For EU product safety concerns, contact us at Calle de José Abascal, 56, 1°, 28003 Madrid, Spain, or email eugpsr@cambridge.org

Youth Culture and Religion in Twenty-First Century Japan

From Hyper-Real to 2.5-Dimensional Religion

Elements in New Religious Movements

DOI: 10.1017/9781009550239
First published online: December 2025

Satoko Fujiwara
University of Tokyo

Hiroki Miura
University of Tokyo

Author for correspondence: Satoko Fujiwara, fujiwara@l.u-tokyo.ac.jp

Abstract: This Element explores emerging forms of religiosity among Japanese young adults. It argues that existing frameworks are insufficient to capture the nuances of youth religiosity in the Era of Virtuality. It introduces the concepts of "2.5-dimensional religion" and "subjective ritualization" to explain how young people engage with digital, fictional, and embodied practices that blur the boundaries between reality and imagination. Drawing from examples such as *oshi-katsu* (fandom-based devotional practices), 2.5-D musicals, tulpa creation, and anime pilgrimage, it identifies a shift from narrative-based subjective myths to embodied and participatory subjective rituals. It demonstrates the ways that contemporary Japanese youth express their religiosity through affective ties, performative engagements, and layered identities in both physical and digital environments. The Element contributes a new theoretical lens for understanding religion across cultures in an age defined by fragmented identities, technological mediation, and the search for connection through affectively charged, often playful, (quasi-)religious practices.

Keywords: Japanese youth culture, fandom, virtuality, postmodern religiosity, mixed reality (MR)

© Satoko Fujiwara and Hiroki Miura 2025

ISBNs: 9781009550260 (HB), 9781009550222 (PB), 9781009550239 (OC)
ISSNs: 2635-232X (online), 2635-2311 (print)

Contents

1 Introduction   1

2 From Hyper-Real to 2.5-Dimensional   15

3 From Subjective Myths to Subjective Ritualization   34

4 Conclusion   52

References   58

Youth Culture and Religion in Twenty-First Century Japan 1

1 Introduction

The 2020 Akutagawa Prize, the most prestigious literary award in Japan, was awarded to 21-year-old Rin Usami[1] for her novel *Oshi, Moyu* (*Idol, Burning*) and its portrayal of a high school protagonist's *oshi-katsu* – activities to express one's support for one's favorite people or things, most typically pop idols. *Oshi-katsu* is part of the subculture known as *otaku* culture in Japan. *Otaku* refers to fans of Japanese subcultures such as anime, manga, and idols, often termed geeks or nerds. The market for *oshi-katsu* expanded during the pandemic years of 2020–2022. A January 2025 survey found that 11 percent of Japan's population and 56 percent of women aged 15 to 19 engage in *oshi-katsu*, spending approximately 3.5 trillion yen annually on these activities.[2] The following excerpt is from Usami's novel. *Oshi* refers to the object of one's intense affection or enthusiasm, and in this context it refers to a male idol singer:

> Each time the group released a new single, I displayed the CD on the shelf that in fandom [*otaku*] circles was known as a "altar."[3] ... The center of this room was obvious from the moment you stepped in. Like the cross inside a church, or the main deity in a temple, a big signed photo of my oshi was displayed on the highest shelf, and around it an array of posters and photos spread across the walls, framed in subtly different shades of cobalt, indigo, teal, and sky blue. The shelves were packed with DVDs, CDs, magazines, and flyers in chronological order, stacked up in layers like geological strata....
>
> I couldn't manage life the way everyone else easily seemed to, and I struggled with the messy consequences every day. But pushing my oshi was the center of my life, a given, and my one point of clarity. It was more than a core – it was my backbone. (Usami 2022: 369–82)

The term "altar" is used metaphorically here (see Figure 1). *Otakus*, the novel's protagonist, and even the author Usami are well aware that *oshi-katsu* is not religion in the conventional sense. However, they overlay religious behaviors on *oshi-katsu*, conscious of its quasi-religious nature. Moreover, for the protagonist, *oshi-katsu* is an absolute anchor of her existence.

---

[1] In this Element, names are presented in the US convention, that is, given name followed by family name (First Name Last Name), unless otherwise noted.
[2] The second survey on *Oshi-katsu* Practices, conducted by CDG Inc. and Oshicoco Inc., targeting 23,000 men and women aged 15 to 69 living in Japan, https://prtimes.jp/main/html/rd/p/000000069.000025413.html (last accessed on March 30, 2025).
[3] The original Japanese word "saidan" is closer in meaning to "altar" than to "shrine," which is the term the translator chose.

Figure 1 *Oshi-katsu* altar. Fictional image created by Fujiwara through AI-generation.

Traditional religions and spiritual cultures are generally unpopular among Japan's youth today. For example, a survey conducted annually since 1995 by Kokugakuin University and the Japanese Association for the Study of Religion and Society targeting university students consistently shows that only about 10 percent of respondents identify with a specific religion such as Christianity or Buddhism (Hirafuji 2021). The trend of distancing from organized religion is evident in Japan, much like in traditionally Christian nations in Europe. Nevertheless, when asked whether they believe in the existence of "power spots" – energy vortexes – 13.8 percent or those surveyed said that they do, and 36.1 percent think it's possible, which might seem high. However, fewer young people are interested in or practice what is called New Age spiritual culture, spirits, fortune-telling, and healing. Some researchers assert that spiritual culture is not widely practiced across any generation in Japan (Reader 2012: 29–31).

The focus of this Element is *not* to argue that *oshi-katsu* is a substitute for religion or that it performs the functions of religion or that it is a functional equivalent of religion. Describing *oshi-katsu* or *otaku* culture as "like religion" is common among students, the general public, and scholars. Yet, this refers to the unreflective, conventional understanding of the concept. That is, phrases such as "idols are 'gods' to fans" or "idols give 'meaning to life'" merely apply a fixed image of religion to subculture. Rather, we treat certain contemporary religious forms as structurally and affectively resembling *oshi-katsu* – fans' sustained practices of supporting and commemorating a beloved figure – including activities such as maintaining an altar-like display for that figure.

This Element thus proposes that a completely new form of religiosity is emerging among contemporary Japanese youth, distinct from traditional religious meanings and New Age spiritual practices. Previous studies by sociologist Adam Possamai on hyper-real religion (Possamai 2005), Carole Cusack on invented religion (Cusack 2010), and Marcus Davidson on fiction-based religion (Davidson 2013) address phenomena that blur the lines between the religious and the secular, and between serious belief and play. Japanese examples of such phenomena – such as Trekkies, Jediism, and the Church of Flying Spaghetti Monster – are subjects of this Element. The cases examined here also occupy an intermediate position between religion and the secular, and between seriousness and play. They have another intermediate characteristic, however, that involves young people engaging with and manipulating spaces that are hard to define as either this world or the other world, and as either real or virtual.

To describe this ambiguous spatiality, we use the term "2.5-dimensional," originating from Japanese *oshi-katsu* culture, signifying a midpoint between the 2-dimensional (manga and anime) and the 3-dimensional (real human activity). When an *otaku* says, "my wife is 2-dimensional," they mean they harbor romantic feelings for a character from manga or anime. Initially an emic term among *otakus*, 2.5-dimensional now has a scholarly definition: "2.5-dimensional culture is a cultural practice that occurs at the ambiguous boundary between the fictional worlds of manga, anime, and games, which prioritize visual information, and the 'real' world, where physical experiences are shared" (Sugawa 2024: 8). Simply put, 2.5-dimensional refers to the realization of 2-dimensional content such as manga, anime, and games in the 3-dimensional space of the human body.

A typical cultural product described by the term 2.5-dimensional is the 2.5-dimensional musical, which involves human actors performing stories from manga and anime. Of course, plays, TV dramas, and films based on manga and novels have existed in great numbers up until the twenty-first century, so the mere act of humans performing anime stories might not seem particularly new. However, the current developments have been specifically named 2.5-dimensional because they necessitate a new concept due to the novel ways fans perceive and interact with space. This will be detailed in the main discussion, but in this Element, the term 2.5-dimensional is used not only for 2.5-dimensional musicals and similar cultural expressions but also expanded beyond its usage in Japanese to denote the uncertain spatiality between dimensions. In other words, this term is used to describe how contemporary young people navigate between virtual reality, augmented reality, and physical reality.

Therefore, we argue that the religiosity of Japan's youth in the 2020s, known as Generation Z,[4] is better captured by the concepts of 2.5-dimensional and "mixed reality" than by Possamai's earlier concept of "hyper-real," and similarly, by the concept of "subjective rituals or ritualization" than by Possamai's "subjective myth" (Possamai 2005). *Oshi-katsu* is also a subject of this Element, although religious and spiritual phenomena that share characteristics with *oshi-katsu* culture are of greater importance to the sociology of religion. We do not claim that "*Oshi-katsu* is like religion," but rather, examine the emergence of religions similar to *oshi-katsu*. We believe that such a perspective is effective not only for analyzing new forms of religiosity in Japan but also for understanding these phenomena in other countries and regions.

Our discussion intersects with the Western sociological study of nonreligiousness and nones. Many young people engaging in religious practices that are neither traditional religion nor spiritual in the conventional senses consider themselves nonreligious. However, we do *not* adopt arguments such as: "they think they are nonreligious, but in fact, they are influenced by Japanese animism or shamanism. *Oshi-katsu* is a manifestation of such religious traditions." We take a post-discursive turn in religious studies and assert that it is meaningless for researchers to make definitive judgments about whether "this is religion" or "that is not religion." Therefore, while the title of this Element is indeed "Youth Culture and Religion" and we have used the phrase "contemporary youth religiosity," the cases discussed include secular instances that are generally not classified as religious. This involves a fundamental issue, discussed elsewhere (Fujiwara & Miura 2024), that historically the relationship between religion and the secular has been reversed in Japan and Europe.[5]

This Element developed out of five "Religious Studies Seminars" held at the University of Tokyo between 2012 and 2024. The authors are the

---

[4] Encyclopedia Britannica defines Generation Z as those individuals born at the end of the twentieth and into the early twenty-first centuries, noting that some sources provide the dates of 1997–2012, www.britannica.com/topic/Generation-Z.

[5] Our argument is that the relation between "religious" and "secular" has been historically reversed in Japan compared to Europe. In Europe, religion was once public through the state-church system, and the secular gradually came to dominate the public sphere under secularization. By contrast, in Japan (and East Asia more broadly), institutionalized religions such as Buddhism were historically private choices, while the public sphere was governed by diffuse social norms with vague supernatural underpinnings. Thus, what counted as "religion" in Europe does not map neatly onto Japan, where public social norms functioned religiously but were not identified as "religion" in the European sense (Fujiwara & Miura 2024: 17–19).

instructor who offered the course (Fujiwara) and one of the students who attended (Miura). The instructor posed this question to the students: "If you think that well-known religious organizations and spiritual cultures are for older people or baby boomers and irrelevant to you, what then is the nature of your religiosity as part of Generation Z? If it is neither religious nor spiritual, how would you articulate it?" This Element originates from this question and is the outcome of the research and discussions that followed.

We begin in the following subsection by outlining a six-part typology of contemporary Japanese youth religiosity, highlighting the first four aspects – practicing belonging, vicarious spirituality, gendered fetishism, and parody of religion – as the background conditions in which newer forms take shape. Section 2 then turns to the fifth aspect, "2.5-dimensional" religiosity, examining how practices such as musicals, fandom, tulpas, and digital experiments embody the ambiguous space between fiction and reality in what we call the Era of Virtuality. Section 3 addresses the sixth aspect, "subjective ritualization," showing how young people move from narrative-based modes of meaning-making to embodied and participatory rituals that sustain affective ties and layered identities. Finally, our conclusion draws together these discussions to argue that Japanese youth religiosity in the 2020s cannot be adequately understood through existing categories such as hyper-real religion, but rather requires new concepts attuned to virtuality, embodiment, and the pluralization of both realities and selves.

Six Aspects of Contemporary Japanese Youth Religiosity

There are three aspects of contemporary Japanese youth's religiosity or nonreligiosity: "practicing belonging," "vicarious spirituality," and "gendered fetishism" (Fujiwara & Miura 2024). Additionally, the "parody of religion" has become an increasing aspect. The themes of this Element, "2.5-dimensional" and "subjective rituals or ritualization," constitute the fifth and sixth aspects. Therefore, while this Element focuses on 2.5-dimensional and subjective rituals or ritualization, we consider that the novelty of the cases presented arises from the combination of these six aspects. In other words, the fifth and sixth aspects that we are introducing cannot be fully understood in isolation. The preceding four aspects form the social and affective conditions in which these new forms emerge. The participatory and affective bonds fostered through "practicing belonging" underpin the immersive engagements of 2.5-dimensional culture, while the supportive dynamic of "vicarious spirituality" parallels the relational orientation of subjective ritualization. "Gendered fetishism" and "the parody of religion" feed into the playful yet affectively charged boundary-crossing practices we examine in the sections that follow. Therefore, let us first briefly explain these four other aspects.

Practicing Belonging

"Practicing belonging" is a concept inspired by Grace Davie's famous notion of "believing without belonging" used to describe nonreligiousness in Europe (Davie 1990). Davie's "believing without belonging" has sparked similar concepts such as "belonging without believing" to articulate nonreligiousness in Europe. However, these expressions are insufficient to describe nonreligiousness in Japan, because even fundamental vocabulary like "God," which is the central object of belief in Western Christian contexts, often means something different in Japan.

Let us provide an example. One of the authors participated in a workshop held in Tokyo in 2019 titled "What would happen if AI became God?" The event was organized by a limited liability company that plans events. It was led by a Japanese artist in his twenties, Yū Amemiya, who calls himself an "experience writer" who writes stories of imaginary worlds and opens them up to real experiences. The participants were about fifty people, mostly men and women in their twenties and thirties. They were divided into groups of five to six and discussed the question "What would happen if AI became God?" The moderator, Amemiya, asked the participants to "first share an understanding of what 'God' means within your group, then discuss what would happen if that AI became such God."

Readers of this Element are undoubtedly familiar with the "singularity discourse"[6] in Western societies over Artificial Intelligence: What will happen if AI's intelligence surpasses that of human beings and becomes God-like? Will it create a utopia because AI will create the best possible world? Or will it turn into a dystopia where humans become slaves to AI? Such discussions are predicated on the notion of the existence of God as an omnipotent and omniscient being who governs the world.

The discussion in the group one of us joined did not go that way at all, however. First, everyone introduced themselves and none professed

---

[6] The term "singularity" or "technological singularity" refers to the hypothetical point in time when AI systems become capable of improving themselves without human intervention, leading to an exponential and uncontrollable growth in their capabilities. "Singularity discourses" revolve around the potential consequences of reaching this point of superintelligent AI.

adherence to a specific religion; all declared themselves nonreligious. Next, they shared what they thought "God" was and what kind of being it might be. They variously said, "God is someone you make requests to," "My grandma says there are seven gods in a single grain of rice," and "When I was a child, I was told not to do bad things because God is watching." But when it came to discussing what would happen if AI became such a God, everyone began to feel puzzled. They were unsure of the intention behind the question and what exactly was being asked.

Unable to bear the confusion in the group, I suggested, "When people say AI becomes God, doesn't that mean it can reliably fulfill your wishes without fail? That AI understands the optimal state for each of you better than you do, and can actually realize it, right?" Their responses were, "Hmm, I think I'd prefer a God who can make some mistakes and seems more relatable than a God who can do everything," and "A God who doesn't necessarily fulfill our wishes but encourages us is good enough."

Then, when I pressed, "So, what do you think the world would be like if AI became such a God?" they thought for a moment and then answered, "It wouldn't be much different from now." Later, when it was time for the full assembly, each group presented their discussion findings, and it turned out that all groups had similar thoughts. In response, Amemiya, the moderator, concluded the discussion by declaring, "The God of the future is a 'sympathetic God'!"

The workshop participants were people who had previously attended events organized by Amemiya or their friends, and although the theme this time was "What if AI became God," they were not particularly interested in religion. Therefore, it would be appropriate to say that their views fairly reflect the general perception of God among contemporary Japanese youth.

We developed the expression "practicing belonging" to describe the religiosity of Japanese youth who identify themselves as nonreligious. In this context, belonging does not refer to belonging to a church, but rather to having connections or relationships with certain groups or individuals. For today's youth, becoming part of groups on social media or fan groups engaging in *oshi-katsu* serves as their place of connection to others, their place of belonging, rather than traditional groups based on geographical or familial ties. In the late twentieth century, joining new religious groups – or what Japanese scholars call new-new religious groups – was one option for young people seeking such a place. However, the 1995 sarin gas attack on the Tokyo subway by Aum Shinrikyō led to the word "religion" acquiring connotations of a dangerous cult in Japan, and those who believed in religion came to be seen as strange. Against this backdrop, more young people started seeking their place of belonging outside religious groups, and the internet facilitated the formation of such connections. The terms "connection" or "belonging" also gained market value. During the time of the Aum Shinrikyō incident, Japanese youth were oriented toward high-end brands in fashion and cars. In contrast, today's Generation Z has a weak desire for brand consumption. The marketing industry identified the replacement as to what they consume as "connection/belonging consumption." This term refers to consumer behavior where individuals may settle for fast (inexpensive) fashion brands of clothing, but spend money to connect with others and boost their spirits by participating in events. Amemiya's company is an example of a young entrepreneur's venture that caters to this connection/belonging consumption desire.

Why do young people seek connection or belonging? It is said that they seek empathy from others and affirmation of themselves from others.[7] When Amemiya said, "The God of the future is a 'sympathetic' God," the term sympathy used here is precisely in this context. Sympathy along with terms such as recognition and desire for recognition have been frequently used since the 2000s, especially the 2010s, and have become terms that symbolize the current era. The Japan of the 1980s and 1990s, when brand consumption flourished during the bubble economy and Japan was touted as No. 1 in business and technology, was a time when Japanese youth enhanced their self-esteem. The spiritual culture in Japan during this period imported the American Human Potential Movement, focusing on boosting personal abilities and achieving self-realization. The 1995 publication *New Age Workshop Catalog* by a Japanese company named Fila Projects, listed about fifty workshops and seminars on spiritual self-improvement methods from the United States (Fila Projects 1995). In contrast, Japan's self-help books in the 2020s have shifted toward not striving, not aiming higher, not seeking material things, but rather pursuing subjective happiness through self-sufficiency, a type of "subtractive self-improvement" (Manabe 2024: 3–5, 26–7). Yasushi Koike, a sociologist of Japanese therapy culture, called this a shift from a "strong self" to a "weak self" (Koike 2007). Today's young people, originally having a weaker sense of self-affirmation, do not seek to maximize their potential but rather use the acceptance of their actual selves by others and empathy for their hobbies as support for their ego. That is why they seek connections: they need others to affirm their self worth.

---

[7] In Japan, there is an abundance of research literature on this subject (Ōta 2007; Furuichi & Honda 2010; Yamatake 2011; Saitō 2013; Nishio et al. 2015).

Figure 2 Shibuya Halloween Party 2017. Photo used by permission courtesy D. T. Johnson.

Practicing belonging refers to ritualistic practices that create such connections. Examples we have used previously include the Halloween parties at the Shibuya Scramble Crossing and the connection-style weddings initiated by the wedding industry in the 2010s (Fujiwara & Miura 2024). The Shibuya Halloween party, before COVID-19, had swollen to hundreds of thousands of participants and was a spontaneous festival for young people, where they enjoyed the night not only with friends but also with people they met there (see Figure 2). Connection-style weddings emerged as a novel style after the increase in Christian-style weddings in Japan since the 1980s. These weddings were marketed as an opportunity to reaffirm connections with people who have supported one's life, such as family and friends, and to seek their recognition of the marriage through unique ceremonies. It was not merely an initiative by the wedding industry; the media also reported that contemporary weddings tended to emphasize dependence on and close relationships with parents over independence and self-reliance among young people (*Asahi Shimbun*, July 20, 2013).

In practicing belonging within religious contexts, people seek connection with divine entities more than salvation. Since around 2014, there has been a "*goshuin* boom," where people collect stamps in a dedicated notebook – called a *goshuincho* – from shrines and temples they visit (see Figures 3 and 4). This is akin to a religious passport program. It has spread across generations, not just among the young. Scholar of religion Norichika Horie has made an interesting observation about this.

> The organizer of a "*goshuin* group" has said: "By looking back at the *goshuin*, you can face the gods again and remember the people, landscapes, and food you encountered on your journey. The *goshuincho* contains not just blessings but also memories."

Figure 3 A *goshuincho* cover. Photo used by permission courtesy of Hakaranora.

> Though she mentions "blessings and memories," when actually asking visitors and sellers of the *goshuincho*, the response is that the real blessing is not the fulfillment of specific prayers but the formation of a tie (*go-en*) with the gods. (Horie 2018: 26; see also Fujiwara 2019)

The "tie" mentioned in this quote means establishing connections. In traditional religious practices, people pray to deities for success in love or business, seeking the fulfillment of their prayers. In the current practice of collecting *goshuin*, value is placed on the act of connecting with the deities themselves. It functions not as a god who grants salvation but as a god who offers sympathy.

This trend does not appear to be limited to Japan. Abby Day has characterized the religiosity of nonreligious young people in England based on interview surveys using the term "believing in belonging." According to Day, people who "believe in belonging … claim social and cultural identities to reinforce a belief in belonging to specific groups of people, particularly those with whom they have affective, adherent relations" (Day 2011: 194). In this example, too, unlike the traditional Christian approach of believing in an absolute God and seeking salvation, value is placed on connecting with people themselves. Day described this as social identity, but in Japan, practicing belonging is a practice by individuals with a "weak self," making the term identity somewhat strong to describe such a mode of being.

Figure 4 A *goshuin* page. Photo used by permission courtesy of Carpegenk.

Vicarious Spirituality

To shed light on this aspect from another angle, we proposed the term "vicarious spirituality," inspired by Davie's concept of vicarious religion (Fujiwara & Miura 2024). Davie used vicarious religion to mean "religion performed by an active minority but on behalf of a much larger number, who (implicitly at least) not only understand, but quite clearly approve of what the minority is doing" (Davie 2008: 169). An example of applying this term to Japan is the analysis that Japanese people prefer Christian-style weddings, despite not being Christians themselves, not just out of a fascination with Western culture but also because they see it as important to have the ceremony conducted by an actual priest or minister on behalf of the nonreligious individuals (LeFebvre 2015: 199–201).

We have discussed how such vicarious phenomena are occurring not only in traditional religions but also in spiritual cultures, using the example of tulpas in Japan (Fujiwara & Miura 2024). Tulpas (see Section 2) originate from Theosophical teachings that draw on Tibetan Buddhism; they are paranormal, sentient beings created by the mind of a meditator.

In Japan, tulpas were adopted by occult practitioners in the 1980s as a type of psychic development to aid their own spiritual growth. From the mid-2000s onward, young people creating tulpas began forming communities on the internet. Analysis of threads from these young people reveals that they are not primarily interested in enhancing their own abilities or achieving self-realization by creating tulpas. Rather, they find fulfillment in helping tulpas grow and develop personalities.

This characteristic is also vividly reflected in Usami's novel *Idol, Burning*. The protagonist, a fan of a male idol, is so devoted to him that "exchanging a few words at a meet and greet [with him] would get me so excited I thought I might explode" (Usami 2022: 628). However, she does not wish to have an actual romantic relationship with him. Instead, she states, "More important, when I pushed my oshi, when I put all of myself on the line and went deep, the commitment might have been one-sided, but I felt more complete than I ever had before" (628). Even if it were possible, she is not seeking self-fulfillment through a romantic relationship. Rather, she finds greater joy in continuously supporting him so that he, as an actor, can achieve self-fulfillment.

We have termed this mentality vicarious spirituality. By comparison, Possamai pointed out the similarity between the human image in the Human Potential Movement and American comic book superheroes, as well as their coexistence (Possamai 2005: 88–101). However, Japanese youth have shifted away from aspiring to become superheroes themselves. As seen in the case of tulpas, this shift is also occurring in the realm of spiritual culture.

Gendered Fetishism

Our third concept, "gendered fetishism," refers to the emotion of *moe* and the practices associated with it in Japanese youth culture.[8] *Moe* is a strong affective, somehow romantic, attachment to an object. In this context, the term fetishism carries both its anthropological meaning of object worship and its psychological meaning of erotic obsession.

One example of this comprises young female *butsuzō* (Buddhist statue) enthusiasts, known as *Butsuzō* Girls (Fujiwara & Miura 2024). These women do not approach Buddhist statues as traditional objects of religious faith but rather seek them in the same way that *otaku*s who love figurines feel *moe* toward them and collect them. Similarly, *moe* is the emotion that young people feel toward the tulpas they create. Most tulpa

---

[8] See Fujuwara & Miura 2024 for further development of the concept of gendered fetishism.

practitioners are male, and it is common for them to have female tulpas as their partners.

Although today's youth are far more accepting of gender and sexual diversity than their parents' generation,[9] and more people question binary gender identities, cultural tendencies show that gender-based distinctions remain. As the media-coined term *Butsuzō* Girl suggests, it is primarily women who experience *moe* toward Buddhist statues. While idol fandom in the 2000s was predominantly associated with male *otaku*, contemporary *oshi-katsu* has developed as a female-centered culture.[10]

The Parody of "Religion"

The three aspects discussed earlier – practicing belonging, vicarious spirituality, and gendered fetishism – illustrate key characteristics of youth culture that are common to both traditionally religious and secular domains. In addition to these, a phenomenon that has been increasing in recent years is the rise of parody religions. It is difficult to categorize parody religions as either religious or secular since they blur the line between serious belief and playful engagement. Mimicking and mocking clergy has existed since premodern times. However, what we see today is a movement that satirizes the very concept of "religion" and engages in "playing religion" (*shūkyō-gokko*).

One of the most representative examples of such parody religions is the Church of the Flying Spaghetti Monster (CFSM), founded in 2005 by Bobby Henderson. CFSM parodies Intelligent Design by claiming that the universe and life were created by the Flying Spaghetti Monster. It spread as a movement opposing the teaching of religiously-motivated pseudoscience in public education. CFSM followers refer to themselves as Pastafarians and conclude prayers using the word Ramen, a type of spaghetti-like noodle, a play on the word Amen, said after Christian prayers. Although Henderson clearly did not intend for CFSM to be taken seriously as a religion (Cusack 2010: 136), it spread rapidly through the

---

[9] Shibuya 109 Entertainment, "Zeddo sedai no jendā ishiki ni taisuru ishiki chōsa (Survey on Gender Awareness among Generation Z)," *PR Times*, https://prtimes.jp/main/html/rd/p/000000108.000033586.html (last accessed on March 30, 2025).

[10] Patrick Galbraith (2019) has analyzed *moe* as the affective engine of *otaku* culture. His ethnography portrays *moe* largely as a male-centered phenomenon oriented toward fictional characters. By contrast, in the 2020s *otaku* and *oshi* culture has become distinctly gendered and diversified. Female fans of male idols and stage actors now gather in Ikebukuro, while Akihabara – once symbolic of male *otaku* identity – has lost its centrality as an "*otaku* town." These shifts indicate that contemporary fan cultures cannot be understood as a homogeneous, male-dominated domain.

internet, eventually "making possible the instantiation of the FSM as the deity of a 'real' religion" (Cusack 2010: 140).

Religions of this kind are unlikely to be recognized as legitimate religions from the perspective of the dominant model of Christianity. Nevertheless, Cusack attempted to classify newly emerging phenomena like CFSM as religions by proposing the framework of "invented religions," which she defined as "not only new but are admitted to be the product of the human imagination" (Cusack 2010: 1). Even if a religion is satirical or parodic, it still provides personal meaning to individuals. "It is reasonable to argue that invented religions look like religions, function like religion, have doctrinal and ritual content that appear religious, and therefore ought to be considered legitimately religious" (Cusack 2010: 148).

An example of a parody religion in Japan is the *MtoP Kyōdan* (MtoP Sect), founded by a young person in his twenties in 2018 and expanded through social media. According to its founder, it was created "as an excuse for taking time off work for 'religious reasons'."[11] The underlying claim is that for nonreligious individuals like him, it is unfair that religious believers can take leave for religious ceremonies, and that current laws unjustly favor those who practice a religion. Of course, in reality, no one (presumably) has successfully taken paid leave by claiming to be a follower of the *MtoP Kyōdan*, nor is the founder attempting to register it as a religious corporation. It remains more of a humor-driven social experiment.

However, other similar religions have emerged, and in 2024, the *Suyasuya Kyō* (Sleep-Soundly Sect) gained media attention. This group upholds the doctrine of "Get proper sleep," treating sleep as a sacred ritual. It is positioned as a religion that allows adherents to refuse jobs that would reduce their sleep "for religious reasons." Before this, many humor-based religions with names ending in -*kyō* (sect) had existed in Japan. One particularly notorious example was *Kōshin Kyō*, a group that engaged in online harassment under the guise of religion. However, recent parody religions go beyond mere satire and attempt to relativize the concept of religion itself and offer a form of social critique. In this respect, they resemble the founder of the CFSM, although CFSM followers in Japan generally have little understanding of its ideological basis – the critique of Christian creationism. Instead, their primary activity on social media consists of sharing reports about where and how they ate ramen.

---

[11] "MtoP Kyōdan," https://mtop.live/ (last accessed on March 30, 2025).

In any case, parody religions can be seen as examples of reflexivity, a characteristic of modernity, extending to the concept of religion itself. Just like adherents of the CFSM, those who create parody religions in Japan initially approach them as satirical pranks. Precisely because they are "pretend" religions, however, their creators become increasingly immersed in making them appear like real religions. This, in turn, makes it difficult to determine whether they are sincerely believed or not. This paradoxical mentality has been described by the Japanese sociologist Masachi Ōsawa as "ironic immersion (devotion)," which he identifies as a defining characteristic of *otaku* culture (Ōsawa 2008: 105). *Otakus* are fully aware that the worlds of anime are fictional, yet they behave as if they are real and immerse themselves in them. Similarly, Jolyon B. Thomas refers to the ambiguous religiosity of today's youth – where it is unclear whether they are genuinely believing or just playing – as "tongue-in-cheek religion" (Thomas 2015).

The four characteristics discussed so far highlight aspects of Japanese youth culture that are difficult to categorize as either religious or secular. Building on this, the next section will explore the fifth characteristic: 2.5-dimensionality.

2 From Hyper-Real to 2.5-Dimensional

As background to the fifth aspect of youth religiosity in Japan – 2.5-dimensional – we begin by examining the shift that has taken place from the postmodern culture of the 1970s to the present. Jean Baudrillard's theory of simulacra (1994) exemplifies this shift, which underpins Adam Possamai's theory of hyper-real religion. Hyper-real religion is a concept that has been widely accepted among scholars of the sociology of religion. Using examples such as Jediism, Possamai defines it as follows:

> By hyper-real religion I thus refer to a simulacrum of a religion partly created out of popular culture which provides inspiration for believers/consumers at a metaphorical level. This religion is still embryonic at the moment, however we can expect a growth of the near future as we move towards a post "September 11th 2001" risk society. (Possamai 2005: 79)[12]

The era indicated by Baudrillard's terms simulacrum and hyper-real corresponds, in the Japanese context, to what sociologists Munesuke Mita and Masachi Ōsawa have called the Era of Fiction or Fictionality. Ōsawa

---

[12] Possamai later modified the definition as: "A hyper-real religion is a simulacrum of a religion created out of, or in symbiosis with, commodified popular culture which provides inspiration at a metaphorical level and/or is a source of beliefs in everyday life" (Possamai 2012: 20).

positioned Aum Shinrikyō as both a typical and extreme example of the culture of the Era of Fiction. We argue that Japanese society has since moved into what we call the Era of Virtuality. Previously, we did not distinguish clearly between fictionality and virtuality (Fujiwara & Miura 2024), and translated Mita and Ōsawa's terminology as Era of Virtuality. We have since come to believe, however, that Era of Fictionality is the more accurate translation. In other words, our argument that Japanese youth culture has turned from hyper-real religion to 2.5-dimensional religion is, at its core, an argument about a broader cultural transition from the Era of Fictionality to the Era of Virtuality. As will become clear, this cultural shift also reconfigures the relationship between the virtual and the material, laying the groundwork for the overview we will draw at the end of this section.

It should be noted that this move – from hyper-real to 2.5-dimensional religiosity – does not occur in a vacuum. It builds on patterns already present across the six aspects of youth religiosity outlined earlier, combining modes of belonging, vicarious engagement, gendered attachment, and playful religiosity in new spatial and technological contexts.

From the Era of Fictionality to the Era of Virtuality

According to Mita and Ōsawa, the Era of Fictionality refers to the period in Japan from around 1975 to 1995. This era follows the Era of the Ideal (approximately 1946 to 1960, Japan's pre-high economic growth period) and the Era of Dreams (approximately 1960 to 1975, Japan's high economic growth period), and corresponds to Japan's post-high economic growth period. The Era of Fictionality aligns with what has also been referred to as the information society, post-industrial society, or consumer society in sociological discussions.

Era of Fictionality and Aum Shinrikyō

In the Era of the Ideal, Japanese youth saw the American lifestyle and democracy as their ideal. During the Era of Dreams, they projected revolutionary dreams onto Marxism and attempted to realize those dreams in the real world. In contrast, the Era of Fictionality refers to a time when young people began to find "meaning in life," not in political ideologies like Marxism, but in fiction, such as manga and anime. Ōsawa identifies Disneyland and *otaku* culture as emblematic of this era and writes:

> The Era of Fictionality is a stage in which people's actions are directed toward constructing, differentiating, enriching, and maintaining a pseudo-reality (fiction) that has been informationalized and codified....

> The Era of Fictionality is symbolized, for example, by (Tokyo) Disneyland (opened in 1983). Disneyland thoroughly excludes external reality through careful design – such as precisely calculating the natural gaze directions of visitors – thereby establishing itself as an autonomous space of fiction (illusion). Its commercial success demonstrates that Japanese society was in the very midst of the Era of Fictionality....
>
> Otaku are people who obsessively and irrationally indulge in what would once have been dismissed as trivial hobbies – anime, video games, computers, idol singers, and so on.... The fields in which otaku immerse themselves are, in many cases, collections of narratives = fictions, as seen most typically in anime. For otaku, it appears that the fictional worlds they love are more important than everyday reality. (Ōsawa 1996: 44–7)

This culture of the Era of Fictionality, in Baudrillardian terms, is a hyper-real culture in which simulacra – corresponding to the Nth generation derivative works[13] in *otaku* culture – become the central mode of artistic expression. In this cultural mode, the distinction between original and copy collapses, and thus the boundaries between true and false, real and imagined, begin to dissolve.

It was during the Era of Fictionality that the "new-new religious groups" emerged, so-called by Japanese scholars in the sociology of religion. In the earlier new religions – such as Sōka Gakkai and Risshō Kōseikai, which expanded rapidly from the end of World War II through the early 1970s – the motivations for joining were often rooted in poverty, illness, and personal conflicts, such as domestic violence. These represented conditions of alienation from the ideal of a prosperous, American-style life, which characterized the Era of the Ideal. By contrast, the motivations for joining the new-new religious groups were more abstract: a vague sense of emptiness or a lack of life purpose. The goal of salvation in the new religions was generally this-worldly benefits. But in new-new religions, the goal shifted to withdrawal from the mundane world. Ōsawa writes:

> The orientation toward withdrawal from the everyday world – reality – is naturally directed toward a certain kind of fiction (a spiritual world), and in doing so, the value distribution between reality and fiction is reversed, placing overwhelming importance on the fictional. Aum Shinrikyō ... is the "typical" example of such a new-new religion. (Ōsawa 1996: 48)

---

[13] "Nth generation derivative work" refers to creative works that are based on previous derivative works, not necessarily made by fans. The second-generation work is the first derivative of the original, and it can inspire a third generation, fourth, fifth, and so on. Collectively, these are referred to as "Nth-generation derivatives," where "N" represents any number in the chain of derivation.

Members of Aum Shinrikyō, who regarded the spiritual world as the true world, sought to bring an end to the real world through an ultimate war, which they called Armageddon, and to build an ideal society composed only of awakened followers. As tensions with society and conflicts within the group increased, members came to believe they were being targeted by evil groups, such as the Freemasons. This conspiratorial fiction – "We are the righteous ones who have seen the truth, and we must defeat the secret powers controlling the world" – was expressed using subcultural forms familiar to members, notably resembling the popular anime *Space Battleship Yamato* (cf. Inoue 2011).

In this way, Aum Shinrikyō was, as Ōsawa argues, a quintessential religion of the Era of Fictionality, in that it found meaning in fiction and expressed that meaning through the medium of anime. However, what distinguished Aum's followers from ordinary fans of Space Battleship Yamato was that they sought to enact the scenario in the real world, ultimately carrying out the sarin gas attack. In this respect, they resembled the youth of the Era of Dreams, who pursued a Marxist scenario and sought to realize it in the real world through revolution. On this point, Ōsawa argued that Aum Shinrikyō was not only a typical example of the Era of Fictionality, but also represented its limit – its endpoint. In other words, the sarin gas attack marked the end of that era. The following subsections will show how the ensuing Era of Virtuality reengages with fiction in materially embodied ways, foreshadowing the hybrid virtual-material forms we later call 2.5-dimensional.

The Difference between Fictional and Virtual

We argue that following the Era of Fictionality, the concept that becomes central in the 2000s is virtuality, as a framework positioned in opposition to "reality." From this perspective, the period since the 2000s can be aptly named the Era of Virtuality. The concept of virtual reality, meaning a reality different from the actual world, had already been popularized by the late 1980s by figures such as Jaron Lanier, considered the founder of the field of virtual reality. Ōsawa also occasionally used the term virtuality, alongside fiction, when discussing the "unrealistic" orientation of Aum Shinrikyō. Indeed, the terms fiction and virtual are sometimes used interchangeably. However, we argue that they can be analytically distinguished as ideal types. While both refer to modes of non-reality, we believe that from the 2000s onward, it is essential to understand youth culture through the lens of virtuality. This is because rapid technological developments in the 2000s brought about widespread use of platforms like Second Life, and in 2021, Meta (formerly Facebook) launched its Metaverse. It also became increasingly common for individuals to own virtual reality (VR) headsets. The technological availability of virtual reality has led to the implementation of augmented reality (AR) – as seen in applications like Pokémon Go! – and the emergence of mixed reality (MR), eventually extending into what is now termed extended reality (XR).

How, then, do virtuality and fictions differ? The virtual refers to entities that have corresponding counterparts in the real world. Examples include churches in Second Life or the Metaverse. These virtual churches are replicas of real-world churches. While they may expand upon the functions of physical churches – such as allowing people to attend the same service while traveling – they continue to correspond to real-world counterparts. In this sense, virtuality enables pseudo-experiences. For example, performing the Hajj (pilgrimage to Mecca) in the Metaverse may not be recognized as an authentic Hajj, but it is accepted as a simulated experience. In this framework, the opposite of the virtual is the real.

In contrast, fictions are creations built entirely from the imagination – constructed from nothing, with complete creative freedom. Fictions need not correspond to the real, and in some cases, their value lies precisely in their distance from reality. In his discussion of the religious use of fiction, Davidsen defines fiction as "any literary narrative which is not intended by its author to refer to events which have taken place in the actual world prior to being entextualised" (Davidsen 2013: 384), emphasizing its non-referential nature. High fantasy works such as *The Lord of the Rings* exemplify this kind of fiction. Furthermore, fiction also carries the meaning of "a lie." In this sense, the opposite of fictions is not the real but the truth expressed through facts – as in the contrast between fiction and nonfiction books. Here, truth is understood as the zero-point, the unaltered state before imagination is applied.

To give a simple example: the story of *Cinderella* is a fiction. Within that story, when Cinderella is transformed through magic and attends the royal ball, that experience can be understood as virtual in the sense of simulated aristocratic socializing – a virtual experience for Cinderella within the fiction.

In this sense, the virtual and fictions differ not only in nature but also in purpose and means.[14] Contemporary phenomena described as virtual

---

[14] We are using the word "fictions" – with an "s" – to indicate a range of imaginary objects (books, movies, television programs, and so on) and belief systems.

are often associated with practical objectives. The Metaverse is a prime example. It provides virtual workspaces, virtual medical training, and the like. Applications like the use of VR headsets in elder care also have practice uses, where caregivers simulate how patients with cognitive impairments perceive the world in order to improve caregiving. Such projects labeled virtual aim to improve society and industry by using innovative technology to manipulate environments and facilitate tasks.

By contrast, fictions do not rely on such technology but instead depend on humanity's ancient capacity for storytelling. As Cusack argues, "play, narrative, and experiences of an order other than the quotidian are central to the emergence and maintenance of religion" (Cusack 2013: 362), and the social construction of a viable worldview becomes possible through imaginative participation in fictional narratives (Cusack 2017: 98). Fictions are primarily created for nonutilitarian purposes, such as entertainment. Strictly speaking, this does not mean fictions lack utility entirely. Yuval Noah Harari uses the term fiction to describe the uniquely *Homo sapiens* ability to imagine shared norms, orders, and worldviews. According to Harari, religion (myth), money, science, nations, capitalism, and communism all fall under the category of large-scale collective fictions.

In short, the virtual is concerned with technology – that is, making something happen – whereas fictions are concerned with narrative – that is, telling a story. To borrow the vocabulary of religion for metaphorical comparison: the virtual corresponds to magic, while fictions correspond to myths. We thus argue that Japan in the twenty-first century should be understood as inhabiting an Era of Virtuality in this very sense. In the subsections that follow, we will see how this era fosters new cultural practices where technological mediation and physical embodiment intertwine.

By calling it the Era of Virtuality, we do not mean that fictions have entirely lost their significance in the 2000s. Beginning slightly before 2020, conspiracy theories – especially QAnon, which spread widely from the United States – also gained traction in Japan. One prominent example was the belief that COVID-19 vaccines were part of a conspiracy orchestrated by major pharmaceutical companies. On platforms like YouTube and other social media, fierce battles unfolded between anti-vaccine conspiracy theorists and science advocates backed by academic authority. Max Weber once described how, in modern society, the domains of economy, politics, art, sexuality, and intellect came into conflict with religion, calling this the "war of the gods" (Weber 1992: 100–1). Today, one might say that a "war of fictions" is underway.[15]

When we turn our attention to youth and *otaku* culture, we do observe a shift from fictions to the virtual. Prior to the Aum Shinrikyō incident, the demand for manga and anime took the form of story, or narrative, consumption. The story of *Space Battleship Yamato*, for instance, was beloved by many fans, and members of Aum Shinrikyō even used its narrative as a model for constructing their apocalyptic scenario. In contrast, from the mid-1990s onward, the nature of *otaku* consumption shifted to what cultural critic Hiroki Azuma called "database consumption" (Azuma 2009 [2001]). According to Azuma, the *moe* feelings that *otaku* experience are not directed toward cohesive narratives, but rather toward individual design elements such as cat ears, maid costumes, or hair springing up like antennae. *Otaku* culture is supported by a vast database of such *moe* elements, from which fans extract and recombine parts to create and enjoy new characters. Azuma described this shift – from the consumption of coherent stories to the combinatorial use of fragmented elements – as a move from story consumption to database consumption.

In the early 2000s, we began to see the emergence of characters created independently of any overarching narrative, constructed within virtual reality that gained widespread fan followings. The most representative example of this phenomenon is Hatsune Miku, the Vocaloid. Hatsune Miku was born from the concept of a synthesized voice made to sing through a virtual girl. She was not based on any manga or anime storyline. As her popularity grew, Miku began performing not only through video streaming on social media but also in live concerts held at real-world venues as a virtual singer. Such phenomena clearly did not exist during the Era of Fictionality.

In the Era of Virtuality, where technology has made virtual reality physically possible, it has become feasible for individuals to exist across multiple realities. The philosopher of social science Alfred Schutz (1899–1959) argued that human beings live while experiencing multiple realities. However, the realities Schutz referred to are those at the level of individual imagination and cognition, such as the world of dreams, fantasy, religious experience, or scientific thought. Among these, he identified the "paramount reality" as the world of everyday life in which social life

---

[15] Some may say that it should be a war *against* fictions because conspiracy theories are fictions while science is not. However, science can also be viewed as a fiction in Harari's sense of the term: a group-shared order and worldview.

is conducted (Schutz 1945). Even in today's Era of Virtuality, a shared physical reality still exists. However, the defining feature of this era's virtuality is that it is often *layered onto* physical reality through the use of technology. As we observed in the earlier VR examples, these experiences are not entirely separate dream worlds disconnected from reality, but rather simulated versions of experiences within the paramount reality. The 2.5-dimensional musicals and tulpas discussed in the next subsection – examples of mixed reality or augmented reality – are even better understood as layers added onto physical reality.

The pluralization of reality goes hand in hand with the pluralization of identity. The subject of the Era of Virtuality possesses multiple identities. This is distinct from the multiplicity of the self as previously conceived in classical sociology – where a person holds various social roles such as father, husband, company employee, or local community representative, and is understood as a node in a network of social relationships. Of course, today's youth may still hold multiple social roles in this traditional sense. However, what characterizes the Era of Virtuality is the tendency to hold multiple accounts across multiple digital platforms, each designed for different purposes, and to construct different identities within each one. For instance: the self represented by Account A on a public-facing social media platform; the self of Account B in a high school alumni network; and the self of Account C in a hobby-based online community. Individuals in this era intentionally switch between these identities, depending on the context.

2.5-Dimensional

A concept that symbolically represents the Era of Virtuality is 2.5-dimensional, a term that began gaining attention in the late 2010s through mass media and has since become the subject of academic research in the context of youth culture. In simple terms, a 2.5-dimensional musical is a stage performance in which actors, dressed in "cosplay"[16] as manga or anime characters, act out scenes from the original works. Described this way, it may not appear particularly novel. However, Tōko Tanaka, who studies 2.5-dimensional culture, explains it differently. She argues that cosplaying actors "actively enter into and immerse themselves in the worldview presented on [the musical] stage, enjoying the overlapping

---

[16] Cosplay combines the words costume and play, and is the term used for creating a costume and dressing up as a fictional character.

Figure 5 2.5-dimensional musical. Fictional image created by Fujiwara through AI-generation.

expression and boundary-crossing between the two-dimensional and three-dimensional realms." She adds:

> These kinds of experiments may be regarded as anticipatory training in bodily techniques for entering and engaging with cross-reality (XR) or mixed reality (MR), where virtual space will be socially implemented and integrated with physical space. (Tanaka 2024: 237)

In other words, the 2.5-dimensional musical itself does not take place within a VR environment like the Metaverse. The use of new technology on stage is limited to features such as projection mapping, which creates background scenery. However, as Tanaka argues, the way fans engage with these musicals – particularly in terms of spatial perception and bodily involvement – closely resembles the kind of experience enabled by XR or MR technologies. To offer a simple analogy: Pokémon GO! corresponds to AR. But if the game were extended into three dimensions, allowing Pokémon monsters to appear as spatially embedded figures within real-world space, it would become MR. This becomes possible when a player wears an MR headset, which overlays virtual space onto the real physical environment. Instead of appearing on a smartphone screen, the Pokémon would appear in front of the player in 3-dimensional space, as seen through the headset. In a similar way, when an actor dressed as an anime character appears on stage in a 2.5-dimensional musical (see Figure 5), the experience for the audience closely resembles that of seeing a 3-dimensional Pokémon appear in their real surroundings. Though not technologically identical, the sensory and perceptual experience is strikingly similar. These qualities – layering fictional worlds onto physical presence, and inviting active audience co-creation – anticipate the broader discussion at the end of this section.

What allows the 2.5-dimensional musical to create an experience so distinct from traditional stage adaptations of novels is that it meets several specific conditions unique to this format. First, the audience consists of fans who are already deeply familiar with the original manga or anime. These fans have a specific *oshi* – a character they are emotionally invested in – and before even watching the musical, they are already able to visualize each scene in three dimensions within their minds. One of the producers of a 2.5-dimensional musical explains this phenomenon as follows:

> When people say "it's like they stepped out of the manga," they're not just talking about appearance. That sense comes from the fact that these originally two-dimensional characters, drawn in pictures, have already been brought to life and given form in the minds of the audience…. That's exactly what we wanted to show. A fantasy world made real. The joy of seeing your favorite character sweating, crying, and actually existing in front of you. (Kataoka & Yamada 2016: 78; quoted in Tsutsui 2024: 188)

This deeply embodied, affective familiarity with the original work allows the performance to feel not merely like a representation, but like a manifestation – a crossing over from fiction into reality.

Second, the actors playing the roles are typically unknown. If a well-known actor were cast, their individual persona would overshadow the manga or anime character they are meant to portray. Instead, actors are chosen primarily for their physical likeness to the original characters. However, this does not mean the actors are unimportant to 2.5-dimensional musical fans. Once an actor is cast, fans will return to the theater again and again to watch the same performance, cheering the inexperienced actor on and hoping they grow as performers through the role. This dynamic is captured in the official website for the 2.5-dimensional musical adaptation of *The Prince of Tennis*, which is set in a high school tennis club:

> The cast is selected primarily based on "how closely they resemble the original characters," regardless of prior stage experience. As the performances accumulate, the way the actors grow mirrors the development of the characters who mature through repeated tennis matches. (Tsutsui 2024: 189)

This focus on the actor's growth and self-realization, supported by the fans' emotional investment, aligns with the previously discussed concept of vicarious spirituality. Fans are not simply consuming entertainment – they are supporting and witnessing the journey of becoming of some being they care about.[17]

---

[17] Galbraith emphasizes that *moe* is directed toward fictional characters, defining it as "an affective response to fictional characters" (Galbraith 2019: 82). In 2.5-dimensional

Third, watching a 2.5-dimensional musical requires participation from the audience. This participation corresponds to what communications theorist Henry Jenkins describes as "participatory culture" (Jenkins et al. 2009). Possamai notes that "participatory culture encompasses hyper-real religionists" (Possamai 2009: 91), and the same is true for 2.5-dimensional culture. Audiences do not merely consume content passively; they actively and creatively participate in the musical experience. Because they are deeply familiar with the source material, audience members supplement the performance by mentally filling in details not explicitly shown on stage – such as scene settings or character backstories – thereby making the fictional character appear more vividly real in the body of the actor (Tsutsui 2024: 197). Furthermore, after the performance, fans contribute to the authenticity of the musical by engaging in a wide range of participatory practices: promoting the show enthusiastically on social media, purchasing and customizing merchandise, attending autograph sessions, sending fan letters and gifts, and conveying messages of support to the actors. Through these ongoing acts of devotion, they help to create the musical's sense of "authenticity" – that is, the sense that it truly and faithfully brings the original work to life (Tanaka 2024: 238). As a result of investing not only money but also time and emotional energy, the characters on stage appear to the audience as beings who are both human and fictional, such that the boundary between actor and character becomes indistinguishable.

The characteristic of gendered fetishism is also clearly evident in 2.5-dimensional musicals. First and foremost, this is a predominantly female-centered culture. According to Rūyma Shineha, a sociologist of science who has studied this phenomenon, fans express *moe* not only for the actor's overall appearance – saying things like "he has a good face" – but also for specific parts of the actor's body, such as "he has good knees" (Shineha 2024: 167). Moreover, when fans share such preferences in gatherings with fellow fans – stating things like "he fits my kinks perfectly" – this functions ritually, almost like a religious confession of faith, according to Shineha (176). These fans form what Shineha calls "communities of preferences," and this community is not limited to fans alone. It also includes actors, as well as narratives, character designs, and stage productions, forming what Bruno Latour refers to as an actor-network (Latour 2005). In this way,

---

musicals, however, fans' attachments extend across an additional ontological layer: real actors embody fictional roles. Audience members invest simultaneously in the fictional character and the performer who enacts them, producing a hybrid affective field that differs significantly from the dynamics of earlier *otaku* culture.

gendered fetishism is deeply intertwined with practicing belonging – it is not just about individualized desire, but about forging shared emotional investments and relational networks through embodied fandom.

In this manner, the participatory intensity and affective investment of 2.5-dimensional musicals directly reflect dynamics we have described under "practicing belonging," "vicarious spirituality," and "gendered fetishism." Fans' ongoing support for specific actors, their repeated attendance, and their creative supplementation of performances mirror the same relational and communal logics that animate other domains of contemporary youth religiosity.

The 2.5-Dimensional Characteristics of Tulpas

The tulpa practices found among contemporary Japanese youth are also examples of the pluralization of reality in the Era of Virtuality. These practices involve layering an imagined being onto the physical world, making them emblematic of this era. Originally a concept situated within occult culture, the tulpa has evolved by blending with youth anime and gaming culture, taking on new characteristics in the process. Tulpa practices offer a compelling case for thinking about the religiosity or nonreligiosity of youth in the Era of Virtuality, particularly in relation to MR, 2.5-dimensional characteristics, and the multiplication of identity.

A tulpa is typically described as a personified being that has no physical form – much like an imaginary friend or imaginary companion – but is nonetheless experienced as psychologically and sensorially real. In the early twenty-first century, efforts to create tulpas as companions or friends spread online, and communities of tulpamancers – those who have created tulpas – continue to interact via social media platforms.

The concept of the tulpa has its roots in Tibetan Buddhism, but was introduced to the West through Theosophy as a supernatural being created through imagination. In the early twentieth century, French explorer Alexandra David-Néel (1868–1969) described the tulpa as a visible apparitional form created by the power of imagination, consciously or unconsciously, presenting it to Western audiences as a Tibetan Buddhist concept (Laursen 2020: 163). David-Néel viewed the tulpa as a magical entity and described it as a potentially dangerous presence that could even harm the magician who created it in some cases.

In Japan, around the 1980s, within the broader current of occult culture, the creation of a tulpa as a mystical form of training for awakening was proposed. One practitioner claimed that by concentrating one's thought, one could create a magical double formed from one's aura. Furthermore, he asserted that by developing the ability to manipulate the aura, it was possible to heal illnesses or physical abnormalities (Takafuji 1987). Another practitioner stated that creating a tulpa would lead to spiritual awakening and the ability to grasp universal truths (Saitō 1988).

However, by the twenty-first century, the focus had shifted toward building comfortable, companion-like relationships with tulpas as intimate beings capable of conversation and interaction. Interest in spiritual awakening or supernatural powers had faded. The following statement is from one of the online threads shared among tulpamancers, offering a contemporary explanation of what a tulpa is:

> "Tulpa" is a name borrowed from Tibetan esoteric Buddhism, and refers to a technique and the beings created by it, constructed within the 2chan bulletin board. While generally considered a secret teaching of Tibetan esoteric Buddhism, it has undergone changes before and after spreading on the 2chan bulletin board and has little in common with the original teachings apart from the name.
>
> This is a technique for creating an imaginary persona with whom one can interact as if it were a real entity. With effort, one can even see the imagined persona with their own eyes or hear their voice as if it were real....
>
> The creation of a tulpa mainly involves creating an imaginary persona and conversing with it. By engaging in a conversation with this imagined persona and imagining their responses, one can eventually receive responses as if they were coming from a real entity. Gradually, the tulpa persona is formed, and it may even start initiating conversations on its own or taking actions beyond just talking....
>
> It is also a fact that many people create tulpas, despite much about tulpas being unknown, and gain enjoyment and emotional bonds from it in their daily lives.[18]

Young people do not seem to create tulpas for the purpose of spiritual awakening or the development of supernatural powers. Rather, they seek emotional connections with their tulpas – companions to help alleviate anxiety, stress, and feelings of loneliness, or friends and familial figures with which to share everyday life.

In the process of creating a tulpa, the practice vividly reflects the database consumption characteristic of the Era of Virtuality. When crafting a tulpa, practitioners choose and combine elements such as appearance,

---

[18] "Tarupa to wa (What is a tulpa?)" in "Tarupa o honki de tsukurō to omotteiru matome (Seriously want to create a tulpa, a summary)," atwiki, September 23, 2020. https://w.atwiki.jp/tarupa/pages/163.html (last accessed on March 30, 2025).

Figure 6 From WikiHow, "How to Make Your Own Tulpa." This is an English-language website, but it has recently adopted a Japanese anime-style tulpa as an example. Retrieved on September 30, 2024. www.wikihow.com/Create-a-Tulpa

personality, and speech style from the subculture according to their personal preferences. Often, these elements are drawn from manga or anime characters, making the creation of a tulpa deeply intertwined with youth anime and gaming culture.

Moreover, the contemporary practice of tulpamancy as it has spread through the internet emphasizes its strong MR dimension – specifically, the projection of the created tulpa onto the real world. Tulpamancers use a technique called "visualization" to attempt to overlay their tulpas onto physical reality (see Figure 6). For example, when a tulpamancer perceives their tulpa in everyday life, the tulpa is often situated in a contextually appropriate position – standing on the ground, sitting in a chair, or otherwise integrated into the physical environment. To make the tulpa feel more real, tulpamancers engage in the extension of their sensory perception, including sight, hearing, and touch. Aurally, they interact with their tulpas through conversations, which may be spoken aloud or conducted internally. Tactilely, some report holding hands with their tulpa to feel physical sensation. Through these practices, they aim to endow the tulpa with a tangible sense of presence. This way of perceiving – through the expansion of reality – clearly illustrates the MR nature of tulpas. The imagined being is not simply a mental figure but is experienced as layered onto and integrated with the physical world, reflecting the complex interplay between imagination and sensory reality characteristic of the Era of Virtuality. This interlacing of imagined beings with embodied perception exemplifies the very processes that, as we will conclude, define the 2.5-dimensional space as a frontier of youth religiosity.

An important point here is that the dimensional space in which the tulpa exists is neither the otherworldly realm nor the physical world, but rather a spatially ambiguous domain that we describe as 2.5-dimensional. A tulpa exists only in relation to its tulpamancer and differs fundamentally from spiritual beings summoned from another world through traditional spirit-mediumship practices. A tulpa is generated and sustained by the tulpamancer's consciousness and imagination. It is neither a resident of a spiritual otherworld nor an autonomous supernatural entity. At the same time, because it lacks a physical body, it cannot be considered part of the real world, either. Instead, the tulpa appears in a 3-dimensional form within a sensorially expanded realm, situated in the in-between – an ambiguous zone that is neither fully real nor fully virtual. As a 2.5-dimensional being, the tulpa blends into the layered and pluralized realities that constitute the tulpamancer's everyday life.

The tulpa phenomenon also illustrates the multiplicity of identity in the Era of Virtuality. In tulpa practice, multiple personalities intersect within a single mind. Just as individuals navigate multiple identities across social media platforms in cyberspace, tulpamancers experience the pluralization of selfhood through their relationship with their tulpa. This interaction becomes a lived expression of the fragmented, layered identities that define contemporary subjectivity.

"Phantom Body" in "Digital Nature"

If tulpas are specter-like beings created through the power of human imagination, there is also a Japanese scientist who claims that it is possible to generate a "phantom body" (*yūtai*[19]) through technology. He is Yōichi Ochiai (b. 1987), a scientist, technologist, and artist who leads a lab at a major national university and is also the CEO of a tech venture company. He is a cultural icon among younger generations, and each of his YouTube videos discussing his project "digital nature" has received over one hundred thousand views. He has received numerous international awards in VR-related fields and has been featured in more than 100 media outlets around the world – TV, newspapers, magazines, and online platforms.

His book *Digital Nature* (2018) bears the subtitle: "Wabi and Sabi by Pantheistic Computers that Form Ecosystems." While singularity theory tends to imagine AI as an omnipotent, god-like being, Ochiai's theory religiously frames the expansion of ubiquitous computing as pantheism, hence the "Pantheistic Computers" in the subtitle. Moreover, "wabi" and

---

[19] "Yū" represents a "phantom" or "ghost," while "tai" represents a "body."

"sabi" are concepts known as the spiritual essence of Zen. In 2024, Ochiai went even further – he founded a physical, rather than online, "Digital Nature Shrine" and became its chief priest.

In the 1990s, the scholar of religion Susumu Shimazono coined the term "spiritual intellectuals" (*reiseiteki chishikijin*) (1996: 247) to describe Japanese philosophers and thinkers active then who were deeply involved in New Age culture – figures who might be seen as contemporary versions of D. T. Suzuki (1870–1966).[20] With his pronounced religious sensibility, Yōichi Ochiai could be considered one of the spiritual intellectuals of the 2020s. In fact, there is a growing number of Japanese researchers working with emergent technologies who are beginning to use religious imagination to envision the future of the digital world – often in dialogue with posthumanist thought.

Let us first introduce Ochiai's theory of digital nature, and then explain what he means by the concept of the phantom body. Ochiai himself describes digital nature (originally in English) as follows:

> Digital nature is the new nature; it is a form of nature merging with computers to continue to evolve.
>
> This new evolved form of life, i.e. digital nature, is rebuilding nature to transcend life and death.
>
> It is transforming everything into everything at high speed, which links up to Chinese and Japanese philosophy such as *Kegon*.[21]
>
> When we define digital nature as the new commons it paves a new way for living as nomads in a rich natural environment, which interestingly connects to stationary nomadism seen in the Jomon era.[22]
>
> There, with AI acting as our interpreter, we will be able to facilitate conversation and exchanges, and also an understanding between communities with inclusivity.
>
> I believe that the way of life for people in this age is to embrace a digital nature and transform it in any way that constitutes a sustainable material nature, so that we can share joy and live together.[23]

In the "nature" that fuses with computers, humans and other living organisms are included. Humans, as well as plants and animals, are, at their core, collections of information based on DNA. By merging that

---

[20] See also Inken Prohl (2000) for a critical evaluation of spiritual intellectuals.
[21] The term "*Kegon*" here refers to the teachings of the Avataṃsaka-sūtra (in Japanese, Kegon-sutra).
[22] The Jomon era is the period between c. 14,000 and 300 BCE in Japanese history.
[23] Ochiai's post to X on March 16, 2023, https://x.com/ochyai/status/1636023339285381120.

data with the vast amount of information accumulated in computers, the world becomes a network where organic life and machines (artificial objects) are interconnected through a digital foundation. This is the fundamental concept behind Ochiai's theory of digital nature – the idea of calling this emerging, interconnected world a new kind of nature. Given that personal data is already flowing into the internet in various forms, and that nonorganic objects and machines are increasingly being connected through the Internet of Things (IoT), the worldview proposed by digital nature is not particularly far-fetched. Instead, it reflects a vision of a world in which the boundaries between the organic and the artificial are becoming increasingly blurred – a vision that resonates strongly with the Era of Virtuality.

Ochiai claims that in digital nature, even life and death are transcended, because he envisions a future in which individual consciousness continues to exist as data. In this context, the term "computer" no longer refers to conventional machines, but becomes synonymous with autonomous AI. According to Ochiai, when human consciousness becomes connected with AI and spreads throughout the world, this state can be described – using terminology from Christian cultural frameworks – as pantheistic. Alternatively, using concepts from Chinese and Japanese Buddhism, it corresponds to the idea of *Kegon*, where the distinction between subject and object disappears, and all things interpenetrate and mutually reflect one another. In other words, Ochiai imagines a world in which boundaries dissolve between mind and machine, individual and collective, self and other – an interconnected, consciousness-infused digital ecosystem.

In the latter half of the twentieth century, postmodern thought also advocated overcoming the modern dualisms of subject/object and mind/body. However, such efforts were ultimately limited to epistemological transformations – changes in how we perceive the world. In contrast, contemporary technologists like Ochiai believe that this goal can now be realized ontologically, that is, physically, through the power of technology. In the passage where Ochiai writes that AI will become our interpreter, he does not mean this in the narrow sense of translating between human languages. Rather, he envisions a future in which the states of plants, animals, and inanimate matter are translated into data, allowing this information to be shared. This, in turn, would make it possible to achieve a sustainable material nature.

The nomads referenced in Ochiai's quote correspond to what he elsewhere calls the phantom body. As technology continues to evolve, digital humans – humans as information – will be able to manifest anywhere in the world by traversing cyberspace, even taking on 3-dimensional form. Today, platforms like the Metaverse already allow us to transcend spatial barriers and interact with people across the globe. But Ochiai's idea of the phantom body differs: it is not an avatar appearing within VR, but the appearance of the person themselves in physical reality. In this sense, the phantom body is more 2.5-dimensional than the Metaverse. Ochiai likens it to becoming a phantasm – able to appear here and there, free from spatial constraints, manifesting not virtually but tangibly in the real world.

> The phenomenon in which humans are transformed into information and come to exist beyond the constraints of time and space can be described, analogically, as a kind of "phantom body." Through the three-dimensional rendering of audiovisual data, informationalized humans are endowed with presence, allowing them to transcend the boundaries between matter, people, and machines. They are digital humans, "virtual (substantial)" beings that transcend the "material" limitations of humanity. Informational technology envisions a society where digital humans roam throughout the city like phantom bodies. (Ochiai 2018: 253)

For Ochiai, the concept of virtual does not carry the usual connotations of being an illusion or something temporary. Rather, it signifies substance or essence – that is, the most fundamental part of what it means to be human. In his thought, that essence is information.

Although Ochiai describes the phantom body as something ghost-like, he is not a proponent of a spiritual worldview in which spirit or anima (soul) are considered to exist as metaphysical entities. In fact, his position is quite the opposite. He proposes that human consciousness and the mind can be converted into data, and through this transformation, interpenetrate with machines (AI). In his view, information is a measurable, physical entity rather than a metaphysical soul. Earlier, we described Ochiai as a spiritual intellectual of the Era of Virtuality. This marks a key difference from the spiritual intellectuals of the Era of Fictionality. While those earlier thinkers operated within frameworks influenced by traditional religion or New Age spirituality, Ochiai presents a worldview that is neither traditionally religious nor spiritual, yet not entirely secular or reductionist in the modern scientific sense either. In short, Ochiai's perspective represents a new mode of religious imagination – distinct from both traditional metaphysics and scientific materialism – that seeks meaning and transcendence through information, technology, and the digital reconfiguration of human existence.

The fundamental difference between Ochiai's worldview, as well as 2.5-dimensional culture, and Possamai's concept of hyper-real religion lies precisely in this point. Hyper-real religion theory is grounded in Baudrillard's theory of the hyper-real, which stands in the lineage of semiotics. It is based on the idea that "we are now living in an economy of signs in which signs are exchanged against each other rather than against the real" (Possamai 2005: 24). In this framework, the hyper-real is defined as "a 'non-material,' a de-materialised, concept of reality" and emerges from the condition in which "the real and unreal have imploded, blurring the distinction between them" (24). Put simply, hyper-real religion operates within a world of signs, abstracted from the physical world – a religion of symbols untethered from materiality. By contrast, in the cases of both Ochiai's thought and 2.5-dimensional culture, while the boundaries between real and unreal are similarly blurred, materiality is not discarded. In Ochiai's case, technology makes the boundary between mind and matter fluid in a physical sense. In the case of 2.5-dimensional musicals, it is through theatrical embodiment – actors physically performing fictional characters – that this interpenetration between the material and the imaginary takes shape. In both cases, physicality and presence matter.

Another notable feature of Ochiai's thought and practice is a return to Japanese cultural roots, which is not overtly nationalistic, but clearly emphasizing cultural reengagement. His Digital Nature Shrine is conceived as "a space that fuses digital technology with the syncretic traditions of Japanese Shinto and Buddhism."[24] Within this shrine, Ochiai enshrines Null no Kami (the Deity of Null), based on the concept of null from computer science, and the Object-Oriented Bodhisattva, inspired by Dainichi Nyorai (the Cosmic Buddha), who represents the overall structure of complex systems. Ochiai even conducted the shrine's founding ceremony dressed in Shinto priest garments, performing the ritual himself. This is not only an example of the concepts of ironic immersion or playing (parody) religion, but also reflects a strong turn toward Japanese cultural identity in twenty-first-century youth culture – one that draws not on American films or pop music, but on Japanese-produced manga and anime as core symbolic resources.

In sum, this section has traced the intricate shift from hyper-real engagements to a nuanced, 2.5-dimensional interplay where the virtual and the material converge, reshaping the cultural and religious landscapes

---

[24] "Ochiai Yoichi Jinja o tateru (Yoichi Ochiai Builds a Shrine: The 'Digital Nature Shrine' Enshrining the 'God of Null' and the 'Object-Oriented Bodhisattva')," *ITmedia*, November 11, 2024, www.itmedia.co.jp/news/articles/2411/11/news176.html (last accessed on March 30, 2025).

of contemporary Japanese youth. We have described this shift as a transition from the Era of Fictionality to the Era of Virtuality, reflecting the digitization of culture (moving from narrative consumption to database consumption) and the technologization of society (where technology actualizes postmodern imaginations that transcend the distinctions between subject and object, and reality and the virtual). Young people's exploration of the 2.5-dimensional space, far from being mere sites of escape, represents a new frontier where the boundaries of reality are continuously negotiated and redefined, and one's self is multiplied. As we move into the next section, we will delve deeper into the nuances of how these emergent forms of engagement are not merely passive consumption but active, ritualistic practices.

3 From Subjective Myths to Subjective Ritualization

In this section, we focus on subjective rituals and ritualization as the sixth aspect of the religiosity – or nonreligiosity – of contemporary Japanese youth. We argue that these concepts are more appropriate than Possamai's notion of subjective myths for describing the religious sensibilities of today's Japanese youth, and that this distinction reflects differences in modes of identity construction. In contrast to the identity-affirming orientation of subjective myths, we will show that contemporary Japanese youth, often characterized by what Koike (2007: 9) calls a "weak self," channel their energies into devotion to others through subjective rituals – a pattern that reflects the shift from narrative-driven to database-driven popular culture consumption.

In his theory of hyper-real religion, Adam Possamai introduces the concept of subjective myths. These are narratives that emerge through the "eclectic consumption of popular culture" found across various spiritual groups or online spaces (Possamai 2005: 57). Subjective myths are defined as myths with "relevance to the self only" (24). One of the best-known examples is Jediism, which draws from the Star Wars mythos. Possamai also cites other cases, such as The Church of All Worlds, a neopagan group that incorporates teachings from the novel *Stranger in a Strange Land*, as well as vampire lore, werewolf narratives, and neopagan mythologies based on the consumption of Tolkienian fantasies (58–62).[25]

Possamai notes that even though these are called "subjective myths," it does not necessarily mean that each individual creates a completely

---

[25] Possamai does not entirely ignore the aspect of practice in hyper-real religion. For instance, he notes that certain practices such as magic are present (2005: 62).

unique myth for themselves. Rather, a specific myth may be shared by a group, and meta-consumption – where someone consumes a subjective myth originally created by someone else – is also possible (Possamai 2005: 67). Moreover, hyper-real religion refers not only to spiritual consumers possessing subjective myths derived from the worldview of something such as Star Wars, but also to the way in which these consumers identify themselves with figures such as the Jedi Knights, and through that identification, "develop their self and tap into latent forms of powers from within the self" (79).

We argue, in contrast, that when analyzing the religiosity of contemporary Japanese youth, the concepts of subjective rituals or ritualization are more appropriate than subjective myths. This is because the mode of popular culture consumption has shifted from story/narrative consumption to database consumption. Take the example of the 2.5-dimensional musical. While these musicals are, of course, based on narratives, what matters most to fans is not the story itself – or, in religious terms, not a unified cosmology – but rather, the characters. These characters exist autonomously from any specific storyline and can continue to be depicted as the same person even in entirely different narratives (Tsutsui 2024: 190). To use the words of Azuma, who theorized database consumption, "Consumers imagine characters, rather than stories, as the more fundamental unit [while anime producers] analyze the popularity of certain character types before constructing particular figures that a narrative would require" (Azuma 2007: 39–40). Symbolically, the title of the first book by Akiko Sugawa, a pioneer in 2.5-dimensional culture studies, is *2.5-Dimensional Culture: Stage, Characters, and Fandom*. She argues that the "foregrounding of characters" (and the corresponding backgrounding of storylines) drove the rise of 2.5-dimensional culture (Sugawa 2021).

For international readers, a helpful comparison might be the consumption of Mickey Mouse rather than that of the Star Wars saga. Characters in 2.5-dimensional culture are similar to Mickey Mouse in that they are not tied to any specific narrative. However, while Mickey Mouse lacks clearly defined traits or preferences, characters in 2.5-dimensional culture come with detailed backstories and personalities – what fans refer to as "setting." Because fans seek to build relationships with these characters through distinctive practices, the emphasis shifts from myth to ritual. In other words, rather than drawing meaning from shared narrative cosmologies, fans engage in subjective ritual actions that establish emotional and symbolic ties with characters. Lev Manovich, a prominent critic of

American new media, has similarly argued that digital media strongly exhibits this very phenomenon – the supersession of narrative by the logic of the database (Manovich 2001: 318–22).

At the beginning of this Element, we quoted a passage from Usami's novel in which the protagonist, who engages in *oshi-katsu*, builds an altar in her room to enshrine her *oshi* (idol). In *oshi-katsu*, other ritual-like practices include pilgrimages to places associated with the idol (*seichi junrei*) and birthday festivals (*seitansai*) to celebrate the idol's birth. It has also become common to create plush dolls representing the *oshi* as avatars, take them along on trips, and pose for commemorative photos together – in other words, creating an idol of the idol. Buying multiple tickets and merchandise to support the *oshi* is called offering (*ofuse*), and engaging in good deeds in daily life to improve one's odds in ticket lotteries is referred to as accumulating virtue (*toku o tsumu*). Spreading the appeal of one's *oshi* to others is called proselytizing (*fukyō*). All of these religious terms are part of the emic vocabulary, terms fans themselves use.

Noticing this, Tami Yanagisawa has pointed out that *oshi-katsu* bears similarities to the religious practices of American evangelical Christians, as analyzed by Tanya Luhrmann in her book *How God Becomes Real* (2020) (Yanagisawa 2024). Luhrmann herself, responding to this observation, writes the following in the preface "To Japanese Readers" of the Japanese edition of her book:

> No country gives fandom the kind of importance that Japan does. I've heard that some Japanese fans build altars for their idols, offer birthday cakes on special days, and treat idols as if they were girlfriends or even wives....
>
> On the surface, *How God Becomes Real* is a book about religion. But the mystery that captivated me is far broader than religion itself.... The most important point is that there are specific habits, techniques, and unspoken cultural expectations that help people feel that an imagined other is truly real.... People repeatedly practice interacting with this imagined god, and through that practice, the god comes to feel vividly and unmistakably real.... I believe this book helps people understand how something that is merely imagined can come to feel real in this world. (Luhrmann 2024: iii–iv, translated from Japanese)

It is important to note that the people Luhrmann focuses on – those who experience God as a real presence – are not all Christians, but specifically modern evangelical Christians who attempt to build a daily, personal relationship with God, not as an awe-inspiring transcendent being, but as a friend-like presence. She gives the example of a young woman who "has coffee with Him [God] regularly" (Luhrmann 2022: 48–9). "These churches wanted people to experience God as concretely and as vividly as the earliest Christian disciples experienced Jesus. They set out to teach them how" (49).

What specific kinds of rituals are practiced in *oshi-katsu* that allow fans to experience their idol as a real presence, in a room where the idol physically is not? And what about the religious practices among contemporary Japanese youth that share similar characteristics with *oshi-katsu*?

Rituals that Make the *Oshi* Real in *Oshi-Katsu*

The various activities in *oshi-katsu* that are described using religious terminology are all part of the practice of supporting one's idol. Fans who engage in *oshi-katsu* are not merely passive consumers of their favorite idol's songs or appearances; rather, they actively perform intentional actions to support and sustain the *oshi*. These actions follow shared patterns across fans, forming a recognizable structure within *oshi-katsu* culture.

For example, at *oshi's* concerts or stage performances, supporters gather with colorful penlights, thumbnail images, and cheering fans (*uchiwa*), which they wave in coordinated rhythms to cheer on their idol. When the *oshi* is a member of a group, each color is associated with a particular member of the group. There are commonly understood rules – created and shared among fans – about how to wave penlights and what chants to call. Following these rules makes the *oshi* appear even more captivating to the fan. This is an example of what cognitive scientists refer to as embodied cognition: the idea that one's physical actions deeply influence one's mental state. The ritualized movements and synchronized cheering are not merely expressions of fandom – they are techniques for making the presence of the *oshi* more real.

Japanese cognitive scientists Shinji Miura and Nobuyuki Kawai (2025) conducted an experiment on cheering behavior from the perspective of embodied cognition. In the study, university students were asked to wave penlights toward characters in a boxing match scene from an anime they had never seen before. They were then asked to evaluate the attractiveness of the characters. The characters were categorized into two types: those who were active (aggressively attacking in the match) and those who were inactive (primarily on the defensive). The participants were instructed to wave the penlights in one of two ways: either forward, like striking a drum – a common motion in *oshi-katsu* concerts – or backward, as if tapping their own shoulder. They were unaware of the experiment's purpose and did not know they were "cheering" for the characters – they simply waved the penlights toward the screen.

The results were striking. Only the characters who were active in the match and toward whom the participants waved the penlight forward were rated significantly higher in attractiveness after the experiment. Characters who were inactive, or who received backward penlight motions, showed no change in attractiveness ratings. In short, even without consciously intending to support a character, the act of waving a penlight forward toward an active character made that character appear more attractive (Miura & Kawai 2025). Needless to say, when the target is one's *oshi*, the conscious, deliberate act of waving a penlight or fan (*uchiwa*) becomes a ritual that enhances both the appeal and the perceived reality of that *oshi* (Kubo 2022: 21–3).

Fans often build an altar at home for their *oshi*. This is not simply a place to display merchandise – it is a ritualized act of expressing affection toward the *oshi*, as well as a space for imaginary communication, where fans talk to their *oshi* and imagine being spoken to in return. Below is a guide to building an altar, found on a website that sells *oshi-katsu* goods and accessories:

> STEP 1: Secure a space in your home for the altar
> Decide on an area where the altar will be set up.
>
> STEP 2: Organize your *oshi* merchandise
> By laying out all your collected goods, it becomes easier to envision what kind of altar you want to create. Sorting items by type – such as favorite photos, pin badges, and acrylic stands[26] – makes the process smoother and helps later with arranging the layout.
>
> STEP 3: Prepare stands or display platforms
> To make your favorite goods look even more appealing, selecting the right display stands or platforms is key. For smaller items like acrylic stands or pin badges, having dedicated holders is especially useful. Mix and match different display tools depending on the size and amount of merchandise to craft your own original altar.
>
> STEP 4: Arrange the merchandise
> Place your most important *oshi* item at the center, then surround it with the rest to create a balanced and visually appealing layout. It's also recommended to decorate the altar in line with your *oshi*'s theme or image color.

---

[26] An image or illustration of a character printed on an acrylic board, designed to stand upright for display.

STEP 5: Add decorations around the altar
Once you've arranged your goods, decorate the surrounding area to create an even more captivating space. You might include magazines or concert pamphlets featuring your *oshi* from past events to complete the setting.[27]

The website describes the process of building an altar as "creating your own sacred space at home." The altar is not only a visual focal point but also a personalized sacred space, where affection, admiration, and imaginative engagement come together in a deeply meaningful ritual practice. While the steps outlined earlier for setting up an altar are not particularly complicated – and fans could likely create one without such a guide – turning the process into a method adds a sense of authenticity or "realness."[28] Moreover, fans often take photos of their altars and share them on social media to display and compare with other fans. In doing so, they need this kind of information to balance adherence to shared conventions with personal expression – following the guidelines while showcasing their individuality.

Luhrmann describes religion as a form of "serious play" or "serious play pretend." She argues that the best comparison for having religious faith, or thinking with a faith frame is "play: an as-if frame in which someone acts according to the expectations of the play frame, while still remaining aware of the realities of the everyday world" (Luhrmann 2022: 22). And further:

> When people act within a faith frame, they engage an ontological attitude in which they act as if something were true – that there is an invisible person who loves them or judges them or is willing to protect them – and they seek to take it seriously despite their knowledge that this as-if sits uneasily with the world they see and know. (Luhrmann 2022: 23)

---

[27] "Oshi-katsu de mimi nisuru 'saidan' to wa? (What Is an 'Altar' in *Oshi-Katsu*? A Guide to Making One with Real Examples)," August 22, 2024, https://jandc-supply.com/blog/archives/2383 (last accessed on March 30, 2025).

[28] Typical *oshi-katsu* altars do not closely resemble traditional Buddhist/Shinto altars such as *Butsudan* and *Kamidana* that their parents or grandparents might have placed in their homes. Their shapes are different, and they are more lavishly decorated and more colorful. On the other hand, Hasegawa, the largest company that makes *Butsudan* and *Kamidana*, has recently created and started selling an *oshi-katsu* altar, which is a replica of a *Kamidana*. It is interesting to note that the company does not view such products as blasphemous to the original *Kamidana*. The company says, for justification of their business, "In recent years, among younger generations, opportunities to pray at family altars or visit graves have been decreasing in daily life. With a desire to preserve the culture of prayer, our company has developed the *Oshi-dan*, a space for one's *oshi*, which can serve as a personal identity and a source of comfort. This allows individuals to cherish feelings of respect and gratitude." Hasegawa Inc., "Oshi no tameno saidan 'oshidan' hanbai kaishi! (Sales begin for the altar for your favorite, '*Oshi-dan*')" *PR Times*, October 16, 2023, https://prtimes.jp/main/html/rd/p/000000043.000028816.html (last accessed on March 30, 2025).

Based on this analysis, we can say that fans who liken their actions in *oshi-katsu* to religious practices are immersed in a layered form of "play pretend." They not only act as if their *oshi* visits the altar they have built and watches over them but also act as if what they are doing is akin to what people call religion. In other words, they participate in a double or even triple "as-if" frame, fully immersed in the serious play of both imagined presence and cultural performance.

Possamai characterizes subjective myths in terms of narcissism, referencing French philosopher Gilles Lipovetsky's theory of postmodernity. He argues that Lipovetsky (b. 1944) understood consumption in advanced modern society as being fundamentally "about the construction of individual identity." Moreover, in the era of postmodern individualism that emerged after the 1960s, "the knowledge of oneself is central," and traditional "macro identities" such as class, gender, ethnicity, and religion are no longer as significant as they once were (Possamai 2005: 65). Building on this, Possamai argues that religion in contemporary society is not just subject to individualization, but also becomes a form of narcissistic individualism. However, this narcissism does not entail self-reflection in the classical sense. Rather, Narcissus "stops looking at himself, and instead looks at an image of himself as portrayed and tamed in the media and popular culture: that is, a hyper-real image of himself – a hyper-real subjective myth" (81).

What distinguishes the subjective rituals of *oshi-katsu* from hyper-real subjective myths is that, although fantasy is layered onto the real world, these rituals are not narcissistic. For fans, the world does not revolve around the self – it revolves around the *oshi*. Rather than seeking self-improvement or personal fulfillment, fans find joy in supporting the growth of their *oshi*, in "raising" and nurturing them. Possamai suggested that hyper-real subjective myths provide consumers with ontological security in a post–9/11 risk society (Possamai 2005: 82). These myths, he argues, are not mere forms of escapism from an anxiety-filled reality, but rather acts of life-affirmation, that is, "an affirmation of a desire to live and experience life in a socio-economic and political context that puts people at risk" (82). By comparison, *oshi-katsu* is also often described by fans as their reason for living, and in that sense, it similarly functions as life affirmation. However, as discussed earlier in this Element (p. 8) in reference to Koike and Manabe, contemporary Japanese youth culture is marked by a generally low baseline of self-esteem.[29] Rather than striving

---

[29] In order to illustrate this point, it is worthwhile to mention the boom among Japanese young people of *isekai tensei* ("reincarnation into another world") novels. This genre

for self-enhancement, many young people rely on their *oshi* as a form of emotional support – something that helps them lift their mood each day and continue living, however tenuously.

The protagonist of Rin Usami's novel pushes back against the adults who insist that she should have an actual romantic relationship with an ordinary man rather than being imaginatively involved with an idol. She responds as follows:

> It was tiresome being told I was taken advantage of, when I had no expectation of getting anything in return. My devotion to my oshi was its own reward, and that worked well for me, so I just needed people to shut up about it. I wasn't looking for my oshi to return my feelings. Probably because I didn't even want to be seen or accepted [by him] the way I was now. I didn't know whether he'd feel positively about me if we ever met, and I didn't even think I'd choose to be by his side 24/7 if it were an option. (Usami 2022: 628)

It may come as a surprise, but the protagonist does not wish to have a romantic relationship with her *oshi* – even if that were a real possibility. A normal boyfriend, even one as beloved as her *oshi*, would inevitably involve the risk of hurting or being hurt. For many young people of her

---

became popular around 2005 and continues to flourish two decades later. A common pattern is that a protagonist suddenly and quite accidentally is reborn into a European medieval-style fantasy world, as represented by *Mushoku Tensei* (Jobless Reincarnation) (2012–2015). This genre reflects the "weak self" of Japanese youth because the protagonist in their original world is typically deprived and plagued by low self-esteem, but upon rebirth in another world, they miraculously gain extraordinary powers and live an exciting and fulfilling life. The point is that what transforms their life is sheer luck. They do not work hard to achieve a new life or to gain special powers; rather, their circumstances change quite accidentally. Moreover, in most novels in this genre, this luck is bestowed solely upon the protagonist, not upon others.

This stands in striking contrast to the most popular manga genre of the 1960s–1980s known as supo-kon ("sports spirit," i.e., sports with a never-give-up ethos). Protagonists of this genre – whether young baseball players, boxers, or other athletes – underwent severe daily training and made every effort to become top players. Young readers of that era were encouraged to believe in themselves, with the message that if they persevered, they would surely succeed someday. By contrast, protagonists of *isekai* novels have no hope for the future in their original world, and their fate is determined mostly by luck or misfortune.

Although this genre constitutes no small part of contemporary youth culture, we do not expand on it in the main text because it is fundamentally narrative-driven and therefore appears to contradict our arguments on database consumption and subjective rituals. Nonetheless, it is not difficult to explain why stories matter in this genre: readers presumably project themselves onto the protagonist and vicariously enjoy living a lucky and exciting life in another world. To experience what the protagonist experiences, a coherent storyline is indispensable. By contrast, in *oshi* culture, fans do not identify with their *oshi* or imaginarily experience stardom themselves. Rather, they find meaning and joy in supporting their *oshi* from the outside.

generation in Japan, that kind of emotional vulnerability is a possibility they cannot overlook. As the protagonist puts it:

> Phones and TV screens had a kind of grace built into their separation, like the distance between the stage and the audience. It was reassuring to sense someone's presence at a certain remove, so that the space couldn't be destroyed by interacting directly, or the relationship ruined by anything I did. More important, when I pushed my oshi, when I put all of myself on the line and went deep, the commitment might have been one-sided, but I felt more complete than I ever had before. (Usami 2022: 628)

In his essay *What Does "Oshi" Mean to Humanity?*, which reflects on his own experiences with *oshi-katsu*, Yoshiaki Yokogawa describes his *oshi* as a kind of *omamori*, or protective charm. This metaphor is endorsed by cognitive scientist Namiko Kubo, author of *The Science of "Oshi"* (Kubo 2022: 218–19). An *omamori* is not like a crystal meant to enhance one's power – it is something calm and modest, something that simply offers support. Yokogawa closes his book with the following words:

> I'm sure that from here on out, everyday life will continue to be full of complications – things that don't go well, moments that make me feel like I might break. There will be times when I trip and fall, when I hit rock bottom, when I cry my eyes out in the middle of the night. But even then, I'll have my *oshi* – my little *omamori* – tucked in my chest pocket. And just that is enough to stop the tears, at least for a moment. It becomes a spark of hope that lets me look up, even when I'm at my lowest and can't seem to stand.
>
> In the end, I'm the one who has to face the world – but that *oshi* becomes a single grain of courage that stirs my timid and anxious self to keep going.
>
> I thought I was the one doing the supporting, but before I knew it, it was my *oshi* who was supporting me. Maybe that's what an *oshi* really is.
>
> Life is long and difficult, but with that kind of *omamori*, I feel like I can somehow make it through. (Yokogawa 2021: 254–5)

The mentality reflected here is significantly different from that of the consumers of Western subjective myths that Possamai discusses – such as the young practitioners of Jediism who seek to identify with Jedi Knights and "develop their self and tap into latent forms of powers from within the self" (Possamai 2005: 79; see also Bainbridge 2024). In contrast, Japanese *oshi* culture is not about constructing a self-identity by building self-esteem. There is no "power" presumed to be within the self. When fans buy large amounts of *oshi*-related merchandise or build elaborate altars, these acts are not understood as ways to fulfill personal desires. Rather, they are expressions of devotion for the *oshi*. It is precisely in order to integrate this devotion into their daily lives as routines that subjective ritualization emerges. In our previous work (Fujiwara & Miura 2024), we referred to this aspect as vicarious spirituality, using tulpa practices as an example.

Tulpa Practice as a Ritual of Real-Making

Just as fans engaged in *oshi-katsu* use ritualization to make their *oshi* feel real, tulpamancers also create rituals to experience their tulpa as real beings. In Section 2, we discussed how tulpa-related practices exhibit characteristics of MR. In this subsection, we focus on the ritualistic aspects constructed by tulpamancers – rituals that form the core of how they perceive an extended version of reality.

In order to create a tulpa as a vivid, lifelike presence, tulpamancers engage in various rituals, often referred to as training. A representative example is the ritual practice of conversation with the tulpa. This is a daily ritual for many tulpamancers. In most cases, the conversation is not spoken aloud but conducted internally through imagination. The following is an example of a commonly shared training method for conversing with a tulpa:

> The key to this technique is not to imagine her [one's tulpa] in a "world inside your head," but rather to imagine her layered onto the real world. Picture her standing right in front of you.... And not only do you imagine her, but you also work on "forming her personality" at the same time. You "make her move."
>
> For example, try having a "conversation" with her. Of course, at first, you'll have to come up with "her lines" yourself and smoothly run a two-person conversation in your head. As you get more comfortable, you can start paying attention to the finer details. Even if you're the one thinking of the words, don't forget to "let her speak." … Eventually, you'll start to lose track of whether you're the one thinking and speaking, or whether she is … and before long, she will begin to speak entirely on her own.[30]

At first, it is merely a self-directed internal dialogue, playing both roles in one's mind. But by repeating this while consciously attributing the words to the tulpa, the practitioner attempts to give the tulpa a tangible sense

---

[30] "Tarupa no tsukurikata (How to create a tulpa)" atWiki. This page says "This is a post that was written on the old 2channel bulletin board before the concept of tulpas became popular. The culture now referred to as 'tulpas' on the internet is all based on the following copypasta" and reproduces a post from 2007, https://w.atwiki.jp/tarupa/pages/11.html (last accessed on March 30, 2025).

of presence. This ritual, aimed at achieving autonomous conversation with the tulpa, is referred to within Japanese communities as *kaiwa ōtoka* (conversation automation), and it represents one of the major goals many tulpamancers pursue in the process of creating a tulpa.

Next, let us turn to a distinctive ritual practice related to tulpas known as possession. This practice, newly devised in the 2000s, is closely tied to the characteristics of the internet, the primary space in which tulpa culture has spread. One tulpa guidebook offers the following explanation for tulpa possession:

> As the name suggests, this refers to the act of allowing a tulpa to possess oneself. Taken literally, this implies a spiritual phenomenon in which the tulpa inhabits the body of the tulper [tulpamancer]. However, no clear or universally defined method exists for this practice. Based on observations of many cases, it seems that most tulpers establish this act by convincing themselves that "the tulpa is the one moving me." In fact, when a tulper adopts the persona of the tulpa to engage in online chat, the term "tulpa possession" is commonly used to describe the activity. For this reason, this more interpretive understanding appears to be generally accepted in practice. (Pokkuru 2018: 41)

In typical spiritual cultural contexts, possession is considered an extraordinary act involving communication with spirits from other worlds or extraterrestrial beings. In contrast, within tulpa practice, possession serves as a means of integrating the tulpa into everyday life. A tulpa can engage in ordinary activities such as eating or reading. What is especially distinctive, however, is that through possession, the tulpa can post to online forums or social media in place of the tulpamancer. In some cases, the tulpa may even have its own social media account, use it to post, and interact with other tulpas or tulpamancers. Through this ritual of possession, tulpamancers strengthen their relationship with the tulpa, treat it as a social being, and thus help it grow and evolve.

Luhrmann focuses on how believers cultivate intimate internal relationships with God or spirits, using the term paracosm to describe an imagined world in which invisible others respond. Through ritual practices, believers construct and share a paracosm as "a private-but-shared imagined world" (Luhrmann 2022: 25), within which unseen beings come to be experienced as real. According to Luhrmann, for a "faith frame" to function as a paracosm, it is essential not only that the invisible other is described, but also that it responds – that it is experienced as interactive. "They know that they are not just pretending when the main character of the story begins to talk back in some way" (48).

In tulpa practice, this very responsiveness and interaction are considered central, and a range of ritual techniques are used to support such experiences. Talking with a tulpa and receiving responses, holding hands with the tulpa, exchanging smiles – these gestures of mutual engagement lie at the core of the tulpamancer–tulpa relationship. Within the tulpa community, practitioners actively exchange methods for making the tulpa feel more real. Beyond the training techniques mentioned earlier, other rituals have been proposed – such as writing down dialogue logs in documents or blogs, or creating a *yorishiro* (an object inhabited by a god/spirit, in this case, the tulpa). Through these practices, the tulpa is transformed from a mere product of imagination into a vivid, lifelike presence.

Rituals in Gaming Culture

Subjective ritualization in youth culture is also frequently observed in the realm of gaming. Gaming culture occupies a central place in the everyday lives of Japanese youth, encompassing console and mobile games, as well as multiplayer platforms. It is not only a matter of entertainment but also a social practice, with players forming communities around shared genres, characters, or play styles. From casual smartphone apps to large-scale online role-playing games, gaming has become a space where young people cultivate affective ties and participate in ritual-like behaviors that extend beyond the screen. Within this broad landscape, particular genres and mechanics foster especially vivid forms of subjective ritualization.

Gacha games – a genre of social network games – are particularly popular among Japanese youth. The word *gacha* originally refers to "a kind of vending machine-dispensed capsule toy," akin to a gumball machine but with toys instead of candy. In gaming, the term is used metaphorically to describe a video game that implements the *gacha* machine-style mechanics. *Gacha* games entice players to spend in-game currency to receive a random item or character, essentially functioning as a form of lottery with a high degree of chance and gambling-like appeal. This game mechanism has become increasingly common not only in Japanese games, but also in those produced in China, Korea, and even Europe and the United States.

Among *gacha* game players, some engage in various rituals – *maginai* in Japanese, including spells and magic – in the hope of obtaining their desired item or character. Numerous websites now introduce different kinds of these magical practices. One such example includes the following steps:

1. Wash your hands.
2. On Twitter, tweet your favorite character's name using the full 140-character limit. (It's okay if the tweet gets cut off mid-sentence; either a nickname or the full name is acceptable.)

3. Bow in a *"dogeza"* position (prostration) and pray toward your smartphone or tablet.
4. Pull the *gacha*.[31]

Even more intriguing are cases in which players create rituals inspired by the narrative settings of fantasy-style games. A prominent example is the role-playing game Fate/Grand Order. In this game, the player takes on the role of a Master, a magician who summons Servants and uses their powers to save the world from destruction. The summoning of these Servants functions as the game's *gacha* mechanic. To call forth a desired character, players often perform personalized rituals or charms.

There are two primary types of these rituals. The first involves preparing an object related to the hero upon whom the desired character is based before initiating the summoning. For instance, to summon the character Gawain, players may place books about the Arthurian Legends (since Gawain is one of the Knights of the Round Table) in front of them before pulling the *gacha*. Similarly, to summon the character Ozymandias, players might display a photograph of a statue of Ramses II, on whom the character is based.

A variation of this ritual type includes making a pilgrimage to a location associated with the historical figure the character is based on – considering it a kind of sacred site – and pulling the *gacha* there. Another variation involves preparing images or merchandise of another character with close ties to the desired one in the original lore, then performing the summoning. These rituals bring elements from within the fictional setting into the real world, blending imagination and reality in an embodied, performative way.

Second, there is a pattern of pulling the *gacha* at the right moment when luck is favorable. One example of this is a practice that players refer to as the Fire-Worship Cult (*haikakyō*). This refers to the act of initiating a summons at the moment when the highest-grade character enhancement item – shaped like a flame – is drawn from a separate, free *gacha* system within the game. The name comes from the flame-like appearance of the item, which is interpreted as an omen of good fortune. Another example is known as the 2 A.M. Cult (*gozen niji-kyō*), based on a line spoken by a character from another title in the Fate series, who claimed that 2 a.m. is the optimal time for summoning a desired Servant. Yet another is the rather infamous Left Nipple Cult (*hidari-chikubi-kyō*), which reportedly began when a player – on a whim – tapped the *gacha* button with their left nipple and received a favorable result. After *gacha* players repeated the

---

[31] "Hikiyose? Gacha de hoshii kyara o hiku omajinai! (Attraction? Charms to Pull the Character You Want in *Gacha*!)" https://ameblo.jp/yuelight01/entry-12248936225.html.

act with continued success, the practice spread via the internet as a sort of lucky ritual.

In this way, many of these ritualistic actions stem from the original story setting, and in that sense, they can be seen as instances where fiction is overlaid onto reality and treated as if it holds actual power. This overlapping of fiction onto the real world is what makes it 2.5-dimensional. The spread and sharing of such unique practices among players is also influenced by the phenomenon of going viral ("buzzing") on social media platforms like X (formerly Twitter). Practices that spread quickly are not necessarily the most credible, but rather those that are slightly bizarre, entertaining, or attention-grabbing. These acts are often likened to religions by players themselves, as in the case of the Fire Worship Cult, the 2 A.M. Cult, or the Left Nipple Cult. While there is an element of parody religion to these, it is also true that players genuinely wish to summon their desired characters.

In addition to these wish-making rituals, there are also instances where formal ceremonial rituals are created. The Pokémon Trading Card Game is one such example. Although it is a competitive game, certain actions during a match have become ritualized. Before starting, players are expected to greet each other with a polite *Yoroshiku onegaishimasu* ("Let's have a good match") and shake hands. After the match, they say *Arigatou gozaimashita* ("Thank you very much") and shake hands again. Many rules are designed to prevent cheating, but there are also specific manners, such as clearly announcing moves and effects during gameplay, and refraining from shouting or insulting the opponent. Through these shared rituals, players help form a sense of community among themselves.

A similar shift from narratives to practices can also be observed in the genre of horror. A video game titled *The Exit 8*, released by a Japanese company in 2023, exemplifies this trend. Set in what resembles an underground subway passage, the game has the player wander through an endlessly repeating corridor, searching for anomalies in order to escape. *The Exit 8* gained immense popularity and inspired a wave of similar games.

These anomalies are phenomena designed to provoke a sense of fear in the player. For example, handprints or footprints might appear on the corridor walls, or the eyes of a person in a poster might move. Some anomalies borrow imagery from famous horror films – for instance, the sudden appearance of twin men or a hallway flooding with red liquid evokes *The Shining*. However, what is particularly notable about

The Exit 8 and its imitators is that they lack any explicit narrative. The player is trapped in a subway-like corridor and must identify the anomalies to escape, but there is no story explaining why the anomalies are occurring or why the player is there in the first place. Rather than being scared by a narrative, the player is reacting, intermittently, to elements of fear that are already shared or socially encoded. Earlier, we discussed the concept of database consumption as a key characteristic of youth culture, referring specifically to the vast collection of *moe* elements. In the case of these horror games, it is a database of fear elements that is being consumed.

The presence of an anomaly is not narrated in voiceover; rather, the game is designed so that players must discover it for themselves by paying close attention. In other words, the fear evoked by this horror game does not arise from passively receiving a narrative, but through the player's active engagement in identifying elements of fear. While this may not rise to the level of a ritual, it does align with our broader argument that the shift from narrative consumption to database consumption corresponds a transition from subjective myths to subjective rituals.

According to folklorist Ryūhei Hirota, horror without narrative is a phenomenon increasingly seen in online horror works worldwide in the 2020s. A pioneering example is the viral 2022 YouTube video titled "The Backrooms (Found Footage)." The Backrooms are a fictional space typically depicted as an eerily vast extradimensional maze of empty, monotonous rooms that one can enter by somehow slipping out of reality. The Backrooms originated in the 2010s as part of the spread of eerie images online, collectively referred to as creepypasta. Ordinary users hoping to create horror content began gathering similar images, which came to be known as liminal spaces. The Backrooms video, created by then-16-year-old American Kane Parsons, is framed as a VHS recording made by a filmmaker who accidentally enters the Backrooms in the 1990s and finds himself pursued by a monster. Hirota notes that the video captures several key features that define internet-based horror of the 2020s. Chief among them is the near-total lack of narrative progression – the entire video maintains an eerie, indescribable atmosphere from beginning to end (Hirota 2024: 223).

Anime Pilgrimage

Another well-known example of youth culture as comprised of subjective rituals and ritualization is anime pilgrimage (*seichi junrei*). Anime pilgrimage refers to a form of pop culture tourism in which fans of anime and related subcultures visit real-world locations that appear as settings, backgrounds, or sources of inspiration in their favorite series. Because such behavior resembles traditional religious pilgrimages, young people began calling this practice by that name from around the end of the first decade of the twenty-first century, when this form of tourism started to gain popularity. Anime pilgrimage has since become the subject of academic research by scholars of religion and tourism studies both in Japan and abroad (Andrews 2014; T. Okamoto 2015; Seaton et al. 2017; Imai 2018; R. Okamoto 2019; Nuradi 2024). As in the cases examined earlier, these practices illustrate how database-style consumption fosters personalized yet socially shared rituals, allowing fictional worlds to be overlaid onto everyday life.

The boom was sparked by the 2007 broadcast of the anime *Lucky Star*. In the anime, one of the characters is depicted as a shrine maiden at Takanomiya Shrine, which was modeled after the real-life Saginomiya Shrine located in the suburbs of Tokyo. Fans who noticed the resemblance began visiting the shrine in cosplay, and as the anime's popularity grew, the number of visitors increased. Online, fans actively exchanged information about anime pilgrimage, which in turn inspired similar pilgrimages to locations featured in other anime series. In these cases, the "sacred sites" were not necessarily religious institutions like shrines but included a variety of real-world locations such as train stations, townscapes, specific shops, coastlines, and mountains. Local governments welcomed the influx of young fans and tourists as an opportunity for regional revitalization, often organizing anime-themed events. By the 2010s, mass media began covering the phenomenon, and a March 2012 NHK report estimated the number of anime pilgrims at around one million.

Scholars of religion have analyzed this phenomenon from various perspectives – examining how fans and local residents form a temporary community and hold festivals together through a Durkheimian lens (R. Okamoto 2019: 146–64), or analyzing the *ema* (votive plaques) left by fans at shrines as material culture (Nuradi 2024). However, the primary reason fans undertake anime pilgrimages is not to participate in festivals with local residents or to leave *ema*. Many pilgrimage sites are not religious locations at all. Fans visit these places to experience the augmented or mixed reality aspects of the pilgrimage, that is, 2.5-dimensionality (see Figure 7). Of course, actors dressed as anime characters do not actually appear at these sites. Rather, it is through the fans' imagination that the fictional world is overlaid onto the real world. (In more recent pilgrimages, fans often bring acrylic stands of their favorite characters and place them at specific spots in the real-world location to take

Figure 7 Anime pilgrimage. A fan is looking at an image of a scene from an anime overlaid onto the actual landscape. Fictional image created by Fujiwara through AI-generation.

photos, thereby recreating scenes from the anime in a 2.5-dimensional fashion.) The excitement comes from discovering the real-world spot from a scene in the anime. The act of layering fictional meaning onto physical reality gives depth and richness to each individual's experience of the world. Additionally, there is a gamified aspect to the pilgrimage, akin to orienteering,[32] in which fans enjoy the challenge of identifying obscure locations that others might overlook.

To elaborate further on the aspect of gameplay, Masayoshi Sakai, a scholar of pop culture industries, points out that while anime pilgrimage fans clearly understand that anime is fictional, they enjoy exploring just how meticulously that fiction has been constructed. Of course, film enthusiasts have long visited filming locations since the twentieth century, but in the case of anime, the real-world locations that inspired scenes are not explicitly mentioned in the works themselves. Instead, fans must deduce and discover them on their own. Sharing such findings and personal deductions with others online is also a key part of the experience – something unique to the digital era. It is this sense of investigative play that Sakai highlights as a novel feature of anime pilgrimage. Another important point he raises is that the locations featured in these works are often just ordinary towns in Japan, and the characters themselves are usually

---

[32] Orienteering is an outdoor sport/game that combines racing with navigation. Participants use a map and compass to find their way to a series of checkpoints spread across varied terrains as quickly as possible. It originated in Scandinavian countries and is popular in Japan.

everyday people, like high school students. This relatability makes it easier for Japanese youth to empathize with the characters and immerse themselves in the fictional world layered onto the real one – something that strongly resonates with the preferences of today's young generation.[33]

However, when local governments over-commercialize anime pilgrimage sites in pursuit of economic benefits, some young people begin to feel a sense of discomfort and distance themselves from the phenomenon.[34] This is because rituals must be subjective rituals – practices created by the individuals themselves. Here, let us clarify a bit more what we mean by subjective.

As a point of comparison, we refer to the typology proposed by Ryōsuke Okamoto, a sociologist of religion specializing in the study of sacred sites. Based on the theory of sociologist Danièle Hervieu-Léger (1999), Okamoto classifies sacred sites into four types, according to how the sacredness of the site is legitimized:

(a) Institutional sacred sites, which are designated by historically dominant religions, such as state religions;
(b) Communal sacred sites, supported by smaller social or religious communities;
(c) Event-based sacred sites, which are temporarily created and sustained by people who share a space for a particular event – examples include anime sacred sites and the Burning Man festival in Nevada, United States;
(d) Private sacred sites, which are recognized as sacred by individuals – for instance, a family grave. (R. Okamoto 2019: 157–8)

Indeed, the sacredness of anime pilgrimage sites is not legitimized solely by individuals, but through a kind of mutual validation among many young fans. However, it is significantly different from large-scale, countercultural events like Burning Man. In anime pilgrimage, it is typical for fans to visit sacred sites alone or in small groups of two or three friends, and it does not usually involve moments of collective effervescence. More recently, a popular trend has emerged in which people visit "sacred" spots associated with their *oshi* (idol), often carrying a plushie or acrylic stand of their *oshi* to photograph on-site. This type of pilgrimage is much closer in form to anime pilgrimage. While sacred site maps are collaboratively created by online fan communities, the actual pilgrimage is carried out as

---

[33] *Close-up Gendai*, "Anime o tabisuru wakamono-tachi: 'Seichi junrei' no butaiura (Young People Traveling for Anime: Behind the Scenes of 'Anime Pilgrimage')," NHK, March 7, 2012.
[34] *Close-up Gendai*, "Anime o tabisuru wakamono-tachi."

a deeply personal act. It is for this reason that we categorize anime pilgrimage under subjective rituals. This, in turn, leads us to a broader insight into the nature of religiosity among contemporary Japanese youth – a point we will elaborate further in the concluding section.

This section has demonstrated that the terms subjective rituals or ritualization aptly describe the religiosity of contemporary Japanese youth. It reflects a shift in identity construction. Today's youth do not build their identities simply as a means to boost self-esteem; rather, possessing a form of weak self, they find their purpose in life in supporting *oshis*, whether they are human idols or spiritual tulpas. Simultaneously, the nature of popular culture consumption has transitioned from narrative-driven to database-driven. This consumption is not passive; young people actively create rituals that blur the lines between religious and secular. These rituals bring idols, anime characters, and tulpas into the physical space, making them virtually real entities with whom they interact. This shift from narrative to database consumption is also evident in online gaming and netlore. These insights allow for an analysis where anime pilgrimage is enjoyed as an overlaying of the anime world onto the real world, adding a layer of meaning to the physical realms they visit.

4 Conclusion

Throughout this study, we have argued that Japan's Generation Z (b. 1997–2009) exhibits a form of religiosity that differs not only from that of the Baby Boomers (b. 1946–1964) but also from that of Generations X (b. 1965–1979/80) and Y (b. 1981–1996, also known as Millennials). This religiosity reflects a significant sociocultural transformation: the "opposite of reality" has shifted from fiction to virtuality. We have used the case of Japan to illustrate how this shift is embodied in a movement from hyper-real religion to 2.5-dimensional religion, and, further, from subjective myths to subjective rituals and ritualization.

To demonstrate this shift, we identified subjective rituals and ritualization as practices that differ from subjective myths. Rather than affirming identity through imagined grand narratives, youth today engage in small-scale, repeatable acts – supporting their *oshi*, visiting anime pilgrimage sites, or interacting with digital companions – that provide orientation and meaning in everyday life.

We also highlighted the framework of 2.5-dimensional culture, where fictional and virtual characters are brought into real-world spaces through performance, media, and fan practices. This cultural environment enables young people to invest emotionally in characters and idols in ways that blur traditional distinctions between the religious and the secular.

Finally, we showed how these practices function as emotional support for youth who often struggle with low self-esteem. Rather than striving for self-enhancement, many find purpose and motivation in sustaining the growth of their *oshi* or maintaining ties to virtual others. These relationships provide not only personal affirmation but also shared social worlds through fandom and online networks.

Taken together, these three patterns suggest a significant transformation: from hyper-real religion rooted in postmodern narratives toward a ritualized religiosity shaped by database-style consumption, affective attachment, and virtuality. By focusing on subjective rituals, 2.5-dimensional culture, and emotional economies, we have sought to identify what is distinctive about the religiosity of Generation Z in Japan.

As with any generational theory, there is an inherent risk of falling into stereotypes. We fully recognize this risk, and we acknowledge that there are many exceptions even within Generation Z. Nevertheless, we have deliberately adopted a generational approach. The reason is that when exploring forms of alternative religiosity that go beyond traditional or institutional religion, relying too heavily on the concept of spirituality risks tethering our perspective to that of Baby Boomer-era New Age culture or New Religious Movements scholarship. As a result, there is a danger of overlooking new forms of religiosity emerging among today's youth. In other words, if we start with the question "What has become of New Age spirituality in the 2020s?" or "How are new religious movements evolving today?," our vision is already constrained from the outset. We may fail to detect entirely new phenomena developing outside those established categories. For this reason, we adopted a generational approach as a heuristic method – a strategy with the potential to break through these limitations and reveal the most recent forms of religiosity arising in our time.

As another strategy for broadening our perspective, we have drawn more heavily from the theories of sociologists, psychologists, and culture critics who analyze contemporary society, rather than relying solely on theories and studies from the field of the sociology of religion. In *Religion and Advanced Industrial Society* (1989), James Beckford identified the problem of the sociology of religion becoming isolated from broader debates in the social sciences (Beckford 1989: 13–17). He argued that the field's dominant theories were developed to analyze industrial societies and had become outdated for understanding religion in *advanced* industrial societies.

Building on this, Inger Furseth and Pål Repstad have pointed out that this situation has changed little even today (Furseth & Repstad 2021: 2). Since the 1960s, many advanced nations have transitioned into advanced industrial societies; the 2020s, marked by further developments in IT, AI, and globalization, demand even newer social theories. Both this Element and our previously published work reflect this view in the selection of theoretical frameworks we have chosen to utilize.

What we have discovered is not necessarily limited to Japan; it is highly likely that similar phenomena can also be observed among young people in other countries and regions. To facilitate future comparative research, we conclude with some theoretical reflections on our findings.

Azuma (2009) and Possamai (2005) both addressed the same historical moment – the era of Gen-X youth shaped by postmodernism. While Possamai's framework has largely given way in Japanese contexts, Azuma's argument remains valuable. His analysis of the "animalization" of *otaku* and the shift from narrative-driven to database-driven consumption continues to illuminate youth culture well into the first two decades of the twenty-first century. Since the task of scholarship is not only to identify historical shifts but also to explain why they occurred, we refer to Azuma's account of animalization as one key to understanding why these new forms of religiosity have taken shape.

Azuma, who proposed the theory of database consumption, emphasizes not only Jean Baudrillard's notion of the simulacrum but also Jean-François Lyotard's postmodern argument about the collapse of grand narratives in the post-1990s era. According to Azuma, this new age is marked by the loss of a single, overarching social norm, replaced by countless smaller, fragmented norms. The internet provides the clearest example: rather than being governed by a hidden, unifying layer of meaning, it functions as a decentralized "database," where users selectively construct their own surface expressions from an accumulation of encoded information (Azuma 2009: 31–2).

From this perspective, contemporary pop culture operates through a "database model," in which cultural products are no longer valued primarily as unified narratives but as collections of reusable elements – character settings, visual motifs, and affective cues such as *moe* or fear[35] (Azuma 2009: 61–2). These elements, designed to trigger strong and immediate emotional responses, form the raw material of postmodern culture. Azuma

---

[35] Azuma (2009) does not explicitly discuss fear. We extend his argument by pairing fear with *moe*, based on our earlier discussion of the horror game genre, where affect operates in a manner analogous to what Azuma describes in relation to *moe*.

describes this shift in terms of "animalization," drawing on Alexandre Kojève to contrast human desire, which depends on intersubjective recognition, with animal needs, which can be satisfied in isolation. In his view, *otaku* consumption increasingly reflects the latter: young people pursue immediate affective gratification, moving rapidly from one set of components to another without the mediating framework of shared narratives or enduring desires (Azuma 2009: 87–8). Nevertheless, Azuma also underscores that this does not eliminate sociality altogether. Rather, it reconfigures it. Youth sociality is increasingly sustained through the exchange of information and affect, rather than through the binding necessity of kinship or community. These connections remain fluid, easily entered into but also easily abandoned – a freedom to "opt out" that has become emblematic of post-1990s society (Azuma 2009: 93).

Our analysis shows how this broader condition of database consumption and animalization has developed in specific directions among contemporary Japanese youth. Rather than remaining enclosed in isolated cycles of gratification, many young people channel their energies into subjective rituals – supporting their *oshi*, visiting anime pilgrimage sites, or sustaining fan practices that overlay fictional worlds onto daily life. These practices extend Azuma's insights but also move beyond them: affective consumption has been reframed not only as individual need-satisfaction but as relational, ritualized devotion. What Possamai described as hyperreal subjective myths for Gen-X has, in the case of Gen-Z, given way to ritualized forms of belonging and emotional support that are grounded in 2.5-dimensional culture.

The transformation that Azuma refers to as animalization had already begun with Generation Y, but we argue that it has intensified further with Generation Z. While the *otaku* Azuma referenced were a minority among Generation Y youth, today, according to the survey cited at the beginning of this Element, more than half of teenage girls express *moe* feelings toward their *oshi* in a way similar to *otaku*. The protagonist of Rin Usami's award-winning novel exemplifies this mentality: the desire *not* to have a real romantic relationship with their *oshi* is symbolic.[36] She devotes herself entirely to her *oshi*, thinks about him constantly, finds purpose in supporting him, and feels sustained by his presence. Yet the *oshi* she engages with is a virtual figure she has projected. She

---

[36] To elaborate, while many young people engaged in *oshi-katsu* do indeed have romantic feelings toward their *oshi*, this does not necessarily mean they want to be in an actual romantic relationship with them. It is more accurate to say that they are each consuming an idealized version of their *oshi* that they have constructed for themselves.

consciously constructs her own object of salvation and then receives that salvation exactly as she intended. This is a closed, self-contained need-satisfaction circuit that functions without a true Other. In this structure, emotional gratification is more reliably achieved. Interacting with a real human being – whose feelings may change, who may hurt or disappoint – is far more unpredictable and thus more emotionally risky. The virtual *oshi* is a far more comfortable and controllable source of emotional fulfillment.

Likewise, the practice of creating a tulpa is also self-contained, without the involvement of others. Unlike traditional religions or earlier forms of spiritual culture – where some kind of other being or external energy from another world visits the self, often in unpredictable ways, bringing either fortune or misfortune – the tulpa is created by the practitioner themselves, and the associated rituals are also entirely self-made. A century ago, when the concept of the tulpa gained attention within the context of Theosophy, there were stories of tulpas developing autonomy and at times turning on their creators. In contrast, in contemporary tulpa practices, such cases are rarely reported. And, even if a tulpa were to become malevolent, for today's young people, it would likely still be easier to manage than a real human being.

Possamai argued that hyper-real religion – that is, the religiosity of Generations X and Y – was likely a product of the risk society that emerged after 9/11 (Possamai 2005: 79–83). We argue that, for Japan's Generation Z, the primary perceived risks lie not in terrorism, large-scale human-made disasters, or natural catastrophes, but rather in close interpersonal relationships. One way of avoiding such risks is through 2.5-dimensional religion – something familiar, situated between reality and fiction, and unlikely to bring unexpected negative consequences. A frequently-cited point in international comparisons is the high rate of non-marriage among Japanese youth. According to the 2018 survey on "Attitudes of Young People in Japan and Other Countries" conducted by Japan's Cabinet Office, the percentage of young Japanese without romantic partners was the highest among the countries surveyed: South Korea, the United States, the United Kingdom, Germany, France, and Sweden. Moreover, the number of such young people continues to increase each year. Among unmarried individuals who are not currently in relationships, nearly half expressed interest in dating, but those who responded "not particularly interested" have also been steadily increasing (Amitani & Nakajima 2021). While this trend cannot be attributed to a single factor, it is clear that more and more young people are choosing not to take the risks associated with close human relationships.

In countries outside Japan as well, it has become a topic of discussion in the 2020s that members of Generation Z tend to have insecure "attachment styles."[37] In an era dominated by social media, Generation Z is more connected than ever – yet many still struggle with deep feelings of insecurity, fear of abandonment, and anxiety in relationships. The American bestseller *The Coddling of the American Mind: How Good Intentions and Bad Ideas Are Setting Up a Generation for Failure* (2018) discusses Generation Z's culture of "safetyism" – a tendency to prioritize safety, including emotional safety, above all else (Lukianoff & Haidt 2018). In Japan, this trend became especially pronounced in the early 2000s, giving rise to the *oshikatsu* boom and accelerating the decline in marriage rates.

We have also argued that in the age of 2.5-dimensional religion – the Era of Virtuality – both reality and identity become pluralized for each individual. This multiplicity of identity is also closely tied to risk avoidance. In cyberspace, people maintain multiple accounts across different platforms for different purposes, switching between identities depending on context. By dispersing their identities in this way, individuals can minimize the emotional damage if something goes wrong with one account or relationship. In Japan, young people refer to these multiple identities as *kyara* (short for "character"). These are self-designed personas, not entirely unique but rather aligned with familiar stock characters from youth culture. Like changing masks to suit different situations and social groups, switching *kyara* is a strategy for reducing interpersonal friction and navigating life more smoothly.

In our view, for Generation Z, religion and spirituality function not as fundamental principles that unify their entire personality, but rather as one among many *kyara* identities they adopt. Because these identities are interchangeable, a religious identity is not more important than a secular one – it stands on equal footing. From this perspective, it becomes clear that forcing research subjects into the traditional binary of religious versus secular, and focusing solely on the former, risks narrowing our vision in the study of religion today.

---

[37] N. Issa, "Young people aren't connecting. Here's why that's a bigger problem than you think," *Deseret News*, May 26, 2023, www.deseret.com/23644088/insecure-attachment-style/;
 "What is your 'attachment style'?: Gen Z's new obsession," *The Times*, December 16, 2023, www.thetimes.com/life-style/health-fitness/article/what-is-your-attachment-style-gen-zs-new-obsession-f2kwqkb0n;
 A. Srivastava, "Understanding anxiety attachment syndrome: A Gen Z guide," February 19, 2025, www.linkedin.com/pulse/understanding-anxiety-attachment-syndrome-gen-z-guide-srivastava-fcuvc (last accessed on March 30, 2025).

References

Amitani, R. & Y. Nakajima. 2021. "Mikonsha no 'izure kekkon shitai' wa naze jitugen shinai noka (Why Do Unmarried People's 'I Want to Get Married Eventually' Not Come True?)." Research Group Report on Population Dynamics and Changes in Economy and Society, Ministry of Finance. www.mof.go.jp/pri/research/conference/fy2020/jinkou_report08.pdf

Andrews, D. K. 2014. "Genesis at the Shrine: The Votive Art of an Anime Pilgrimage." *Mechademia* 9: 217–33. http://doi.org/10.1353/mec.2014.0001

Asahi Shimbun (newspaper). 2013. "Saishinban kekkonshiki to fūfu no katachi: Oya, yūjin tono 'kizuna' jūshi (Latest Edition: Forms of Marriage and Couples – Emphasizing Bonds with Parents and Friends)," July 20, morning edition, 4.

Azuma, H. 2007. *Gēmuteki riarizumu no tanjō: Dōbutsuka suru posuto modan 2 (The Birth of Game-Like Realism: The Animalization of Post-Modernity 2)*. Tokyo: Kodansha.

Azuma, H. 2009. *Otaku: Japan's Database Animals*, trans. J. E. Abel and S. Kono. Minneapolis: University of Minnesota Press. Originally, H. Azuma, Dōbutsuka suru posuto modan: Otaku kara mita nihon shakai (The Animalization of Post-Modernity: Japanese Society from an Otaku Perspective). Tokyo: Kodansha, 2001.

Bainbridge, W. S. 2024. *The Sacred Force of Star Wars Jedi*. Cambridge: Cambridge University Press.

Baudrillard, J. 1994. *Simulacra and Simulation*, trans. S. F. Glaser. Ann Arbor: University of Michigan Press.

Beckford, J. 1989. *Religion and Advanced Industrial Society*. London: Routledge.

Cusack, C. M. 2010. *Invented Religions: Imagination, Fiction and Faith*. New York & Abingdon: Routledge.

Cusack, C. M. 2013. "Play, Narrative and the Creation of Religion: Extending the Theoretical Base of 'Invented Religions'." *Culture and Religion* 14, no. 4: 362–77. https://doi.org/10.1080/14755610.2013.838797

Cusack, C. M. 2017. "Fiction into Religion: Imagination, Other Worlds, and Play in the Formation of Community." In M. A. Davidsen, ed., *Narrative and Belief: The Religious Affordance of Supernatural Fiction*, 87–102. London & New York: Routledge.

References

Davidson, M. A. 2013. "Fiction-Based Religion: Conceptualising a New Category against History-Based Religion and Fandom." *Culture and Religion* 14, no. 4: 378–95. https://doi.org/10.1080/14755610.2013.838798

Davie, G. 1990. "Believing without Belonging: Is This the Future of Religion in Britain?" *Social Compass* 37, no. 4: 455–69. https://doi.org/10.1177/003776890037004004

Davie, G. 2008. "From 'Believing without Belonging' to 'Vicarious Religion': Understanding the Patterns of Religion in Modern Europe." In D. Pollack & D. V. A. Olson, eds., *The Role of Religion in Modern Societies*, 165–76. New York: Routledge.

Day, A. 2011. *Believing in Belonging: Belief and Social Identity in the Modern World.* Oxford: Oxford University Press.

Fila Projects. 1995. *Nyūeiji wākushoppu katarogu (New Age Workshop Catalog)*. Tokyo: Fila Projects.

Fujiwara, S. 2019. "Practicing Belonging?: Non-religiousness in Twenty-First Century Japan." *Journal of Religion in Japan* 8, no. 1–3: 123–50. https://doi-org.utokyo.idm.oclc.org/10.1163/22118349-00801008

Fujiwara, S. & H. Miura. 2024. "Practicing Belonging, Vicarious Spirituality, and Gendered Fetishism: The Transformation of the Non-religious/Religious in Contemporary Japanese Youth Culture." *Social Compass* 71, no. 2: 212–35. https://doi.org/10.1177/00377686241260494

Furseth, I. & P. Repstad. 2021. *Modern Sociologists on Society and Religion.* New York: Routledge.

Furuichi, N. & Y. Honda. 2010. *Kibōnanmin goikkōsama: Pīsu bōto to "shōnin no kyōdōtai" gensō (Here Are Refugees in Search of Hope: Peace Boat and the Illusioned "Community of Mutual Recognition")*. Tokyo: Kōbunsha.

Galbraith, P. W. 2019. *Otaku and the Struggle for Imagination in Japan*, Kindle ed. Durham, NC: Duke University Press.

Hervieu-Léger, D. 1999. *Le Pèlerin et le converti: La religion en mouvement.* Paris: Flammarion.

Hirafuji, K. 2021. "Daijūsankai gakusei shūkyō ishiki chōsa hōkoku (Report of the 13th Student Religious Consciousness Survey)." The Institute for Japanese Culture and Classics, Kokugakuin University.

Hirota, R. 2024. *Netto kaidan no minzokugaku (The Folklore of Internet Ghost Stories)*. Tokyo: Hayakawashobō.

Horie, N. 2018. "Dentō kaiki? Soretomo chihō shōmetsu? (Return to Tradition? Or the Disappearance of Local Communities?)." In N. Horie, ed., *Gendai nihon no shūkyōjijō (Religious Landscape of Contemporary Japan)*, 25–34. Tokyo: Iwanamishoten.

Imai, N. 2018. *Otaku bunka to shūkyō no rinkai (Boundary between Otaku Culture and Religion)*. Kyoto: Kōyōshobō.
Inoue, N., ed. 2011. *Jōhō jidai no Aum Shinrikyō (Aum Shinrikyō in the Information Age)*. Tokyo: Shunjūsha.
Jenkins, H., R. Purushotma, M. Weigel, K. Clinton, & A. Robison. 2009. *Confronting the Challenges of Participatory Culture: Media Education for the 21st Century*. Cambridge, MA: MIT Press. https://direct.mit.edu/books/oa-monograph/3204/Confronting-the-Challenges-of-Participatory
Kataoka, Y. & N. Yamada. 2016. "Purodeusā to mangaka ga kataru, 2.5 jigen myūjikaru no gentaiken (A Producer and a Manga Artist Discuss the Original Experience of 2.5-Dimensional Musicals)." *Bijutsu techo*. Tokyo: Bijutsu Shuppan, July, 76–81.
Koike, Y. 2007. *Serapī bunka no shakaigaku (Sociology of Therapeutic Culture)*. Tokyo: Keisōshobō.
Kubo, N. K. 2022. *"Oshi" no kagaku: purojekushon saiensu towa nanika (The Science of "Oshi": What Is Projection Science?)*. Tokyo: Shūeisha.
Latour, B. 2005. *Reassembling the Social: An Introduction to Actor-Network-Theory*. Oxford: Oxford University Press.
Laursen, C. 2020. "Plurality through Imagination: The Emergence of Online Tulpa Communities in the Making of New Identities." In S. Natale and D. Pasulka, eds., *Believing in Bits: Digital Media and the Supernatural*, 163–79. New York: Oxford University Press.
LeFebvre, J. R. 2015. "Christian Wedding Ceremonies: 'Nonreligiousness' in Contemporary Japan." *Japanese Journal of Religious Studies* 42, no. 2: 185–203. http://doi.org/10.18874/jjrs.42.2.2015.185-203
Luhrmann, T. M. 2022. *How God Becomes Real: Kindling the Presence of Invisible Others*. Princeton, NJ: Princeton University Press.
Luhrmann, T. M. 2024. *Riaru meikingu*, trans T. Yanagisawa. Tokyo: Keio University Press. Originally, T. M. Luhrmann, *How God Becomes Real: Kindling the Presence of Invisible Others*. Princeton, NJ: Princeton University Press, 2020.
Lukianoff, G. & J. Haidt. 2018. *The Coddling of the American Mind: How Good Intentions and Bad Ideas Are Setting Up a Generation for Failure*. New York: Penguin Press.
Manabe, A. 2024. *Jinsei wa kokoro no mochikata de kaerareru? (Can Life Be Changed by the Way You Set Your Mind?)*. Tokyo: Kōbunsha.
Manovich, L. 2001. *The Language of New Media*. Cambridge, MA: MIT Press.

Miura, S. & N. Kawai. 2025. "Sairium o zenpō ni furuto anime no kyarakutā ni taisuru tsuyosa no hyouka ga takamaru (Waving a Light Stick Forward Increases the Strength Rating of Animated Characters)." *Journal of the Japan Society of Kansei Engineering* 24, no. 2: 229–36. https://doi.org/10.5057/jjske.TJSKE-D-24-00062

Nishio, T., K. Yamaguch, & W. Kusaka. 2015. *Shōnin yokubō no shakai henkaku (Social Upheaval by Desires to Be Recognized)*. Kyoto: Kyoto University Press.

Nuradi, R. H. 2024. "The Anime Network: Materiality in Anime Pilgrimage." *Journal of Religion in Japan* 13, nos. 2–3: 119–42. https://doi.org/10.1163/22118349-01302002

Ochiai, Y. 2018. *Dejitaru neichā: Seitaikei o nasu hanshinka keisanki niyoru wabi to sabi (Digital Nature: Wabi and Sabi by Pantheistic Computers that Form Ecosystems)*. Tokyo: Planets.

Okamoto, R. 2019. *Pilgrimages in the Secular Age: From El Camino to Anime*, trans. D. Iwabuchi & K. Enda. Tokyo: Japan Publishing Industry Foundation for Culture. Originally, R. Okamoto, *Seichi junrei: Sekai isan kara anime no butai made (Pilgrimage: From World Heritage Sites to Anime Settings)*. Tokyo: Chūōkōronshinsha, 2015.

Okamoto, T. 2015. "Otaku Tourism and the Anime Pilgrimage Phenomenon in Japan." *Japan Forum* 27, no. 1: 12–36. https://doi.org/10.1080/09555803.2014.962565

Ōsawa, M. 1996. *Kyokō no jidai no hate: Aum to sekai saishū sensō (The End of the Era of Fiction: Aum and the Final World War)*. Tokyo: Chikuma shobō.

Ōsawa, M. 2008. *Fukanōsei no jidai (The Age of Impossibility)*. Tokyo: Iwanamishoten.

Ōta, H. 2007. *Shōnin yokkyu: "Mitomeraretai" o dō ikasuka? (Desire for Recognition: How to Leverage the Need to Be Acknowledged?)*. Tokyo: Toyokeizaishinpōsha.

Pokkuru. 2018. *Tarupa kakeru konpurekkusu (Tulpa X Complex)*, Kindle ed. Tokyo: Switch.

Possamai, A. 2005. *Religion and Popular Culture: A Hyper-Real Testament*. Bruxelles: P. I. E.-Peter Lang.

Possamai, A. 2009. *Sociology of Religion for Generations X and Y*. London: Equinox.

Possamai, A. 2012. "Yoda Goes to Glastonbury: An Introduction to Hyper-Real Religions." In A. Possamai, ed., *Handbook of Hyper-Real Religions*, 1–21. Leiden: Brill.

Prohl, I. 2000. *Die "Spirituellen Intellektuellen" und das New Age in Japan.* Hamburg: Gesellschaft für Natur- und Völkerkunde Ostasiens e.V.

Reader, I. 2012. "Secularisation, R.I.P.? Nonsense! The 'Rush Hour Away from the Gods' and the Decline of Religion in Contemporary Japan." *Journal of Religion in Japan* 1, no. 1: 7–36. https://doi.org/10.1163/22 1183412X628370

Saitō, K. 1988. "Kyōi no jinkō seimeitai 'tarupa' no sōnen sōzōhō (How to Create Astonishing Artificial Life 'Tulpa' with Thoughts)." *Gekkan Mū (Monthly Mu Magazine).* Tokyo: Gakken, 120–24.

Saitō, T. 2013. *Shōnin o meguru yamai (Disease over Recognition).* Tokyo: Nihonhyōronsha.

Schutz, A. 1945. "On Multiple Realities." *Philosophy and Phenomenological Research* 5: 533–76.

Seaton, P., T. Yamamura, A. Sugawa-Shimada, & K. Jang. 2017. *Contents Tourism in Japan: Pilgrimages to "Sacred Sites" of Popular Culture.* Amherst, NY: Cambria.

Shimazono, S. 1996. *Seishin sekai no yukue: Gendai sekai to shinreisei undō (The Future of the Spiritual World: New Spirituality Movements in the Global Society).* Tokyo: Tokyodō Shuppan.

Shineha, R. 2024. "2.5 jigen kūkan niokeru hyōshō no kansen (The Spread of Representation in 2.5-Dimensional Space)." In A. Sugawa, ed., *2.5 jigen gaku nyūmon (Introduction to 2.5-Dimensional Culture Studies)*, 163–84. Tokyo: Seidosha.

Sugawa, A. 2021. *2.5 jigen bunka ron: butai, kyarakutā, fandam (A Study of 2.5-Dimensional Culture: Stage, Characters, and Fandom).* Tokyo: Seikyūsha.

Sugawa, A. 2024. "Joshō: 2.5 jigen bunka kenkyū no genzai (Introduction: The Current State of 2.5-Dimensional Culture Studies)." In A. Sugawa, ed., *2.5 jigen gaku nyūmon (Introduction to 2.5-Dimensional Culture Studies)*, 7–18. Tokyo: Seidosha.

Takafuji, S. 1987. *Kiseki no sūpā bijon (Miraculous Supervision).* Tokyo: Gakken.

Tanaka, T. 2024. "2.5 jigen myūjikaru to fanbunka (2.5-Dimensional Musical and Fandom Culture)." In A. Sugawa, ed., *2.5 jigen gaku nyūmon (Introduction to 2.5-Dimensional Culture Studies)*, 227–57. Tokyo: Seidosha.

Thomas, J. B. 2015. "Tongue in Cheek, Just in Case." *Sacred Matters Magazine*, June 13. https://sacredmattersmagazine.com/tongue-in-cheek-just-in-case/.

Tsutsui, H. 2024. "Mienaimono o miyō to suru (Trying to See the Invisible)." In A. Sugawa, ed., *2.5 jigen gaku nyūmon (Introduction to 2.5-Dimensional Culture Studies)*, 185–225. Tokyo: Seidosha.

Usami, R. 2022. *Idol, Burning*, trans. A. Yoneda. Kindle ed. Edinburgh: Canongate Books.

Weber, M. 1992. *Wissenschaft als Beruf 1917/1919, Politik als Beruf 1919*. Hrsg. von W. J. Mommsen et al. Tübingen: Mohr Siebeck.

Yamatake, S. 2011. *"Mitomeraretai" no shōtai: Shōnin fuan no jidai (What Is Behind "Desires to Be Recognized": The Age of Recognition-Uncertainty)*. Tokyo: Kōdansha.

Yanagisawa, T. 2024. "Yakusha atogaki (Translator's Afterword)." In T. M. Luhrmann, *Riaru meikingu*, trans. T. Yanagisawa. Tokyo: Keio University Press. Originally, T. M. Luhrmann, *How God Becomes Real: Kindling the Presence of Invisible Others*. Princeton, NJ: Princeton University Press, 2020.

Yokogawa, Y. 2021. *Jinrui ni totte oshi towa nannanoka (What Is "Oshi" for Human Beings)*. Tokyo: Sunmark.

Acknowledgments

We are grateful to Rebecca Moore for inviting us to write this Element for the series and for her invaluable editorial guidance throughout – both in her thoughtful comments on the manuscript and in her careful editorial work. We also thank the two anonymous reviewers for their insightful and constructive comments, which helped us to clarify and strengthen the argument.

Cambridge Elements =

New Religious Movements

Founding Editor
†James R. Lewis
Wuhan University

The late James R. Lewis was a Professor of Philosophy at Wuhan University, China. He was the author or co-author of 128 articles and reference book entries, and editor or co-editor of 50 books. Most recently he was the general editor for the *Alternative Spirituality and Religion Review* and served as the associate editor for the *Journal of Religion and Violence*. His prolific publications include *The Cambridge Companion to Religion and Terrorism* (Cambridge University Press 2017) and *Falun Gong: Spiritual Warfare and Martyrdom* (Cambridge University Press 2018).

Series Editor
Rebecca Moore
San Diego State University

Rebecca Moore is Emerita Professor of Religious Studies at San Diego State University. She has written and edited numerous books and articles on Peoples Temple and the Jonestown tragedy. Publications include *Beyond Brainwashing: Perspectives on Cultic Violence* (Cambridge University Press 2018) and *Peoples Temple and Jonestown in the Twenty-First Century* (Cambridge University Press 2022). She is reviews editor for *Nova Religio*, the quarterly journal on new and emergent religions published by the University of Pennsylvania Press.

About the Series

Elements in New Religious Movements go beyond cult stereotypes and popular prejudices to present new religions and their adherents in a scholarly and engaging manner. Case studies of individual groups, such as Transcendental Meditation and Scientology, provide in-depth consideration of some of the most well known, and controversial, groups. Thematic examinations of women, children, science, technology, and other topics focus on specific issues unique to these groups. Historical analyses locate new religions in specific religious, social, political, and cultural contexts. These examinations demonstrate why some groups exist in tension with the wider society and why others live peaceably in the mainstream. The series highlights the differences, as well as the similarities, within this great variety of religious expressions.

Cambridge Elements ≡

New Religious Movements

Elements in the Series

Jehovah's Witnesses
Jolene Chu and Ollimatti Peltonen

Wearing Their Faith: New Religious Movements, Dress, and Fashion in America
Lynn S. Neal

Santa Muerte Devotion: Vulnerability, Protection, Intimacy
Wil G. Pansters

J. Krishnamurti: Self-Inquiry, Awakening, and Transformation
Constance A Jones

Making Places Sacred: New Articulations of Place and Power
Matt Tomlinson and Yujie Zhu

Korean New Religions
Don Baker

The Revelation Spiritual Home: The Revival of African Indigenous Spirituality
Massimo Introvigne and Rosita Šorytė

Minority Religions, the Law, and the Courts: Cases and Consequences
James T. Richardson

Early Twentieth Century New Black Religious Movements in the United States
Darrius D. Hills

Abuse in New Religious Movements
Sarah Harvey

New Religious Movements and the Romantic Spirit of Modernity
Stef Aupers, Dick Houtman, and Galen Watts

Youth Culture and Religion in Twenty-First Century Japan: From Hyper-real Real to 2.5-Dimensional Religion
Satoko Fujiwara and Hiroki Miura

A full series listing is available at: www.cambridge.org/ENRM

Made in the USA
Monee, IL
03 May 2026

49437836R00042